GOD REVEALED
Revisit Your Past to Enrich Your Future

AMINA

BRUCE HAS FOUND A REAL
GEM TO WORK AS HIS ASSISTANT.
IT WAS A WONDERFUL EXPERIENCE
FOR ME — THANK YOU.

I HOPE YOU ENJOY THE BOOK
AND it ENRICHES YOUR FUTURE

MANY BLESSINGS,

Fred Sievert

"Fred Sievert retired from a successful business career as the highly respected president of New York Life to pursue his deeper passions, including attending Yale Divinity School and writing about his lifelong encounters with God. I have been studying, writing, and speaking for decades about the ways in which longer life affords us second chances and new beginnings. Fred's story is a dazzling example of an individual, who in his post-career life, is attempting to make the transition from success to significance. *God Revealed* is a poignant, thoughtful, and illuminating look into life's deeper meanings and mysteries."

—**Ken Dychtwald, Ph.D.**, psychologist/gerontologist,
founding CEO of Age Wave,
author of *Bodymind, Age Wave, The Power Years*,
and *A New Purpose: Redefining Money,
Family, Work, Retirement and Success*

"Fred's family stories inspired me to write my own family story about God's grace through a painful divorce. My Christmas letter reconnected me with family and friends. You'll be inspired too as you see God Revealed in the stories in this book."

—**Larry Bennett**, past president of the
New York Life Agents Advisory Council

"Through thirty-two refreshingly clear-headed recollections, Sievert engages us in an exploration of faithfulness and the sacred in life. His rich experience of family, business leadership, and personal growth is coupled to a theologically trained approach that challenges him and the reader to discover, listen, trust, and receive the very complicated blessings of faith."

—**Laura Nash, Ph.D.**, coauthor of
Just Enough: Tools for Creating Success in Work and Life;
former senior lecturer, Harvard Business School

"Restless souls in a restless culture we are, and often unaware that our very restlessness is a form of longing for transcendence, for the experience of the Divine. In this book the former president of a major company (rather than a "religious professional") tells his own story with the goal of opening minds and hearts to the possibility of encounters with God in everyday life. Like our loves, our encounters with God are unique to each one of us; and also like our loves, our genuine encounters with God are contagious. The record of Sievert's experiences in *God Revealed* will fascinate and challenge you and stimulate you to think in a discerning way about your life and God's place in it."

—**Miroslav Volf**, Henry B. Wright Professor of Theology,
Yale Divinity School, and founder and director
of the Yale Center for Faith & Culture

"I was in New York City when Fred Sievert spoke to more than 10,000 New York Life agents and employees at Radio City Music Hall. He was electrifying as the leader of a great company. But his greatest inspiration is found in the pages of this book, where he quietly shares the lessons he's learned from listening to the kind and benevolent God who quietly guides our lives. His experiences will remind you of the crucial times when God was part of your life. Draw deeply from this well of inspiration."

—**Jerry Borrowman**, co-author of
A Distant Prayer—Miracles of the 49th Combat Mission
with Joseph Banks, DFC, deceased

"Fred Sievert's book *God Revealed* fits perfectly wherever you are in your own faith journey. While reading, prepare to be challenged, comforted, charmed, and humbled. My own journey through the pages revealed God's presence in my life as I reflected on relationships, crossroads, God's timing, struggles, and joy. Fred Sievert's website, www.godrevealed.com, nourishes my soul; this book provides a wonderful companion as I seek to find passion during retirement years and understand God's purpose for my life."

—**Sue Johnson**, seeker, lifelong learner,
retired teacher, counselor, and school principal

"*God Revealed* is a remarkable and inspiring book that gives us real-life examples of how to watch for and listen to God's guidance in our lives. If the book were only a collection of Fred's memoirs it would be fascinating reading, but it is much more than that. Here Fred challenges us to reflect on our own lives in a way that I found especially meaningful and revealed new truths about my own walk with God."

—**Wendy T. Wallace**, president of Christian Message through Art

"Sometimes it's hard to see God's hand at work; however, looking back, God's fingerprints are often visible everywhere. In order to help us learn how to recognize God in our personal experiences, Fred Sievert has put together this wonderful collection of stories about how God has been revealed in his life."

—**David M. Holland**, retired president and
CEO of Munich American Reassurance Co.

"This honest and engaging book deserves careful consideration by anyone interested in broadening his understanding of the many ways in which God can reveal Himself to us. As President of New York Life Insurance Company, Fred Sievert's enlightened leadership had a positive impact on the lives of many people. He continues on that path by sharing with us this inspiring account of his personal spiritual journey."

—**James L. Broadhead**, retired CEO of NextEra Energy, Inc.

"This book has encouraged me to look at my emerging life experiences from a new perspective. Now, when I don't see or understand God's plan,

I feel cradled in His loving arms despite my lack of insight. Fred's words encourage me to approach each day as if it were a renewed search for God's existence and influence in my life. I find myself looking about in curious wonder while my heart leaps into my voice, saying, 'Here I am.' Thank you, Fred, for the awakening!"

—**Donnah K. Haisley**, owner, designer,
and president of HootieBrown Designs, LLC

This book is one of those rare books that comes along bearing precisely the gift needed at precisely the right time. Whether you are a person of deep faith or a seeker taking your first tentative steps on your spiritual journey, Fred Sievert's remarkable book offers wise and accessible guidance on the way. Spiritual giants and mystics have been blessed with vivid, unmistakable experiences of the God in whom "we live and move and have our being." The rest of us experience intimations of beauty and holiness, comfort and consolation, ambiguous enough to overlook if distracted or careless, clear enough to see if we attend to them with patience and desire. Fred Sievert has been paying attention. In this book he combines a lifetime of careful seeking and reflection, a business leader's concern for clarity and accessibility, and a seminarian's professional grounding in three-thousand years of Judeo-Christian spiritual reflection. His moving testimony to diverse experiences, his rubric of remembrance, reexamination, and reflection, and his practical combination of witness, scripture, and practical exercises are an invaluable lamp onto the feet of people of faith and the congregations to which they are drawn.

—The Reverend **Harold E. Masback, III**
Senior Minister, The Congregational Church of New Canaan

GOD
REVEALED

Revisit Your Past

....

to Enrich Your Future

FRED SIEVERT

NEW YORK

GOD REVEALED
Revisit Your Past to Enrich Your Future

Disclaimer: The Publisher and the Author make no representations or warranties with respect to the accuracy or completeness of the contents of this work and specifically disclaim all warranties, including without limitation warranties of fitness for a particular purpose. No warranty may be created or extended by sales or promotional materials. The advice and strategies contained herein may not be suitable for every situation. This work is sold with the understanding that the Publisher is not engaged in rendering legal, accounting, or other professional services. If professional assistance is required, the services of a competent professional person should be sought. Neither the Publisher nor the Author shall be liable for damages arising herefrom. The fact that an organization or website is referred to in this work as a citation and/ or a potential source of further information does not mean that the Author or the Publisher endorses the information the organization or website may provide or recommendations it may make. Further, readers should be aware that Internet websites listed in this work may have changed or disappeared between when this work was written and when it is read.

ISBN 978-1-61448-699-2 paperback
ISBN 978-1-61448-700-5 eBook
ISBN 978-1-61448-701-2 audio
Library of Congress Control Number: 2013939315

Morgan James Publishing
The Entrepreneurial Publisher
5 Penn Plaza, 23rd Floor,
New York City, New York 10001
(212) 655-5470 office • (516) 908-4496 fax
www.MorganJamesPublishing.com

Cover Design by:
Rachel Lopez
www.r2cdesign.com

In an effort to support local communities and raise awareness and funds, Morgan James Publishing donates a percentage of all book sales for the life of each book to Habitat for Humanity Peninsula and Greater Williamsburg.

Get involved today, visit
www.MorganJamesBuilds.com.

Habitat for Humanity®
Peninsula and
Greater Williamsburg
Building Partner

DEDICATION

....

This book is dedicated to my family: my wife, Sue, and my five children, Heidi, Dena, Denise, Zachary, and Cornell. Each of them has unselfishly endured my workaholic lifestyle for decades and their encouragement and support has continued into my retirement years, during which the intensity only increased.

I especially thank them for allowing me to write about them and how God has spoken to me through numerous familial experiences that intimately involved each of them. This writing project began as an effort to memorialize my encounters with God for their benefit. And, once again, I was driven and consumed by my passionate pursuit of a major project, while they steadfastly supported my every effort. I will be eternally grateful.

TABLE OF CONTENTS

· ·

How to Read
and Get the Most
Out of This Book

··································

This book is ultimately about you, not me. That may seem like an odd thing to say, given the fact that all of the stories that follow are my experiences and the book even reads a lot like my personal memoirs. If that's how you read this book, then you probably will enjoy the stories, you may even become more watchful for God's everyday presence in your life, but you will miss some of the value.

Each chapter of this book and each story within each chapter is meant to be a memory trigger—to trigger your recollection of experiences in your own life. These may be experiences you have not previously realized were packed with divine guidance or intervention. The stories I tell may elicit long-forgotten memories of highly significant events that, when re-examined will give you divine inspiration, help, insights, and more, allowing you to re-experience, through memory, your life in a whole new way.

Each story is followed by a brief "For Reflection" section that is designed not only to communicate the lessons I learned, but also to further jog your memory and trigger a nurturing and clarifying re-experience.

After you have given my story and your elicited memories some thought, you may wonder how this knowledge affects your current and future behaviors. You may even begin searching for ways to act upon what you now see as messages, instructions, or admonitions from God. To facilitate this process, in addition to the reflections that follow each story, you'll find an optional set of exercises at the end of each full chapter.

The final chapter of the book attempts to pull all aspects of your introspection and reflection together by asking three thought-provoking questions about what you have learned and how your life might change as a result of reading this book and examining your past. It will be useful to have these three questions in mind as you read each chapter of the book:

1. How can you be well prepared to experience or hear from God in the future?
2. What have your encounters revealed about the nature of God?
3. How might you respond to messages or guidance from God?

I'm confident that you will have thoughtful answers when you have finished reading the book. And through those answers, may your relationship with God be enhanced.

As the subtitle of the book suggests, it is my prayer and hope that by revisiting your past you will enrich your future.

Chapter Exercises

Each chapter of this book ends with optional exercises. The exercise questions are designed for discussion by a study group but they can just as easily be addressed individually or with a spouse or reading partner. If you prefer not to break the continuity of your reading experience, you may choose to return to the exercises after reading the entire book.

The exercises are designed to make your reading experience more personal, by encouraging you to thoughtfully consider your own historical encounters with God. If you're successful in recalling such experiences, I hope you will then be more comfortable sharing them with family, friends, and acquaintances either individually or in a group setting. Additionally, by completing these exercises, I hope you'll not only touch the lives of other believers, but also be better prepared to more attentively encounter God and experience His love and guidance in the future.

I encourage you to briefly capture your answers to the questions in writing for possible future reference and elaboration as your skills in ascertaining God's presence mature and develop further.

PREFACE

· ·

Nearing the end of my graduate studies in religion at Yale Divinity School, I was filled with questions: How would I ever impact more lives than I had in my former career as the president of a large Fortune 100 company with more than 55,000 agents and employees? Was my voluntary early retirement a mistake? Had I diminished my potential to impact lives by selfishly pursuing my personal development and education at Yale?

As I grappled with doubt, God stepped in and provided the answer at precisely the right moment—through the voice of my child: "Dad," said my daughter, "do you realize you have told your stories to thousands of employees and agents of New York Life but you've never told them to your own family?"

It was August 2009, and I was sitting across from Dena and her husband, Doug, over a gourmet Italian dinner. Throughout the course of that meal, our lively conversation had turned to memories of my long career at New York Life—including the many characters I encountered and the unique experiences I enjoyed. The hours passed quickly as I related story after story, and I was pleased but puzzled to observe the extent of their interest and captive attention. So I was surprised at Dena's insistence: "Dad, at a minimum, you need to memorialize your stories in writing for our benefit."

Her words hit me very hard. She was absolutely right. Once again I had neglected my family in favor of my selfish, dogged career pursuits.

Growing up in a lower-middle-class family, my aspirations weren't nearly as great as my ultimate reality. But the diverse events in my life led to growth, development, and an understanding of how God would ultimately utilize me. Throughout it all, I came to recognize a complex link between anxiety, providential intervention, and divine revelation—which was the essence of the stories I shared with Dena and Doug.

The dinner with my daughter and son-in-law was preceded by more than thirty years of aggressive, ambitious pursuit of an ultimately successful but demanding business career that culminated in my retirement in June of 2007. I was often disillusioned over my purpose in life, but my career was gratifying. I felt I was touching not only the lives of the company's agents and employees but also the lives of its five million customers. After all, New York Life provided death benefits and retirement income to policyholders in their times of greatest need. Knowing that was very important to me, because touching and impacting the lives of others has been, and always will be, my greatest passion.

Then why did I retire early, at age fifty-nine, when I could have continued to fulfill that passion for six more years?

There are many ways to answer that question—but here's what is most important: The intense requirements of my job caused me to severely neglect my family and my spiritual development. Although I was active in my church and though I found some ways to cope with my time constraints, I felt a burning desire to dedicate more focused time to those things that really mattered to me and to my God. Believing that my business responsibilities were the problem, I began planning for my retirement some three years before I actually retired.

My plans included spending more time with my family, pursuing an advanced academic degree in religion at Yale Divinity School, retaining my seat on several nonprofit boards, teaching business school courses, and mentoring a number of young executives. All these activities would give me the opportunity to touch lives in different capacities while pursuing my passions. After my official retirement, I did follow those passions and quickly realized that, for me, "retirement" was a misnomer.

Throughout my long career, I had been a workaholic—and to my initial dismay, that affliction was not instantly cured by my pseudo-retirement. In my planning and doing, in fact, I had ambitiously taken on much more than I could handle in twenty-four hours a day, seven days a week—let alone eight hours a day, five days a week! As a result, the same problems I'd suffered during my career came back to haunt me as I followed my passions into my post-retirement years. My time and neglect problems hadn't been because of the job!

Immediately after dinner with Dena, I went home and began compiling stories. It was a shockingly long list, spanning a wide range of topics and involving an eclectic cast of characters. These were all stories that could help my family and maybe other people. Finding the time to write them would be my challenge.

Until this moment, writing a book had been low on my priority list. Now that it had become important, I knew that the only way I could find time to work was to multitask. Every morning I drafted material in emails to myself on my BlackBerry while riding my stationary exercise bike. Clearly, obsessive-compulsive behaviors were difficult to abandon.

I had lots of topics—but what was the overriding message of the book? Twenty stories later, I was amazed to find that the common theme that tied them together was as plain as day.

Almost every story had occurred at a time when I was struggling with my faith or with a personal, family, or business issue. Until I started writing, I didn't fully realize how God was guiding me. Even though I prayed often in the face of difficult decisions or troubling situations, I hadn't always realized that God was attentive and present in those encounters with family, friends, and even strangers—that at the time seemed completely coincidental.

I kept writing. And the more I wrote, the more obvious it was that God had spoken to me in a way that helped me cope with those faith challenges, personal anxieties, and life issues. *How could I have been so*

busy as to not even recognize that God's hand was guiding me? . . . And how
many other Christians aren't watching and listening for those divine messages
in their lives?

And so this book was born.

ACKNOWLEDGMENTS

· ·

The events of my life that inspired the stories of this book were what I believed to be undeniable encounters with God. Though I am from humble origins and struggled in life no less than most people, it was God's presence and guidance that enabled me to lead a blessed existence, instilling a strong desire to tell my story in hope of touching many lives. It is my daily walk with the Lord Jesus Christ and the indwelling Holy Spirit that has enabled someone like me to stay on the right course and experience a life filled with joy, wonder, and anticipation of even better things to come. Thanks be to God!

The support and encouragement of my immediate family and friends, too numerous to mention by name, is what inspired me to complete this book in the face of many other often conflicting priorities and pursuits. And I would be remiss not to mention my extended family of New York Life colleagues, agents, and employees who gave me incredible support throughout the process and served as a marketing test bed as I shared selected stories with hundreds of them over the course of the past three years.

All of our personal faith journeys are touched by the lives of hundreds of believers with whom we come in contact. The collection of characters noted in this book from presidents of the United States to commoners are just a few who have contributed significantly to my own spiritual development and growth, each in their own way providing opportunities to get a glimpse of God's grace and love.

The amount of work and rework involved in writing and editing a book like this is mind-boggling. I thought I was a reasonably good writer until I sought advice from many of my author friends and then submitted my early versions to my editors. I could never have successfully told my story without the professional advice and editing of many highly competent individuals. In addition to several bestselling authors whom I consulted, I must give credit to my agent Chris Ferebee and to the three editors I used most extensively throughout the process. Rachel Watson brought a scholarly theological perspective to the book and made a significant number of suggested content revisions. Kathy Jenkins and Betsy Robinson went well beyond typical copy editing by embracing the work and reflecting their own strong faith in suggesting numerous enhancements.

And finally I am grateful to all the fine folks at Morgan James Publishing who allowed me to tell my story by taking a chance on an unknown, previously unpublished author who simply wanted to reveal his encounters with God in order to touch more lives.

INTRODUCTION

· ·

The message of this book is simple: God speaks to us in often unanticipated ways, and we need to be attentive to divine intervention and realize what those experiences and messages mean to us. And very importantly, armed with this knowledge, how can we prospectively learn from it and enrich our lives?

My stories do not dwell extensively on my own theological beliefs. *They are not intended to be a prescription for finding your own place in a family of believers.* I came to know God through contemplation, self-study, prayer, and revelation.

To explain my emotions and reactions to my encounters with God, let me tell you a bit about my background and my spiritual formation.

Every life is a unique journey. Mine began like that of millions of other Americans, in an unremarkable and very typical lower-middle-class household. I was born to second- and third-generation European immigrants who worked hard to support and sustain a young family in a rebounding post-World War II economy.

Throughout my childhood, my parents struggled financially. Neither my mother nor my father graduated from high school as they were Depression-era teenagers forced to work to support their families;

that work ethic persisted for the rest of their lives. I took only one short vacation as a child and didn't fly in an airplane until I left home for college. As a result, the formation of my attitude toward money, work, and sacrifice was shaped in ways unlike those of other kids whose parents were much more comfortable financially. For me, pursuit of the American Dream was an early and driving ambition.

My father worked long, hard hours as an insurance inspector. A working-class guy who collected data for low pay, he supplemented his income by following his real passion: playing the trumpet. It was his passion for music—not his work in the insurance industry—that defined him and his life.

His dedication to his passion affected my childhood and my adult life as I identified and pursued my own passions.

Dad had a strong faith in God but rarely expressed it and did not regularly take the family to church. It was difficult for him to express the things he felt strongly about, and he rarely revealed emotions to his family. But as I watched him handle life's challenges, I came to understand the depth of his faith. I would later come to realize how much I was like my dad.

Mom didn't often express her faith either. But she was less guarded with her emotions and did find occasions to express her faith in God and her reliance on His direction and guidance. She too worked several low-paying jobs and she enjoyed being engaged in something productive. She was a lifetime learner, eager to advance her knowledge even as she became fragile and forgetful in her early eighties.

I think my lack of formal religious training had both a negative and a positive impact on the future development of my faith.

On the negative side, I did not affiliate at a young age with any particular body of believers. I did not learn Bible stories, with their inherent wisdom and moralistic values. And I did not have the benefit of worshipping and interacting regularly with other believers.

But there were positive aspects to this background as well. I was not indoctrinated into a narrowly defined religious belief system. I was inspired to pursue my beliefs independently, with an open mind while

I contemplated and considered many difficult theological questions and objectively considered possible answers. And most importantly, God knew I needed divine revelation to fortify my faith.

It was through numerous kitchen-table chats with Mom that I (even as an adult) gained enhanced self-worth and self-confidence. Ironically, although God or religion didn't come up often in those discussions, a lot of moral principles did, and they became embedded in my psyche. Mom always encouraged me to work hard and to do so with integrity. She always emphasized doing what was right. Our chats may not have been formal Bible studies, but Mom often quoted the Ten Commandments and the Golden Rule as principles by which I should live my life. I listened and absorbed what she was saying. I believed her.

Even in the competitive, secular corporate world, I always did my best to follow my mother's advice. I worked very hard, striving to demonstrate integrity while being ever mindful of compassion and the commandments.

Those extremely simple instructions from my parents and their demonstration of how to live accordingly have stayed with me for a lifetime. What a blessing it is to have had childhood experiences that were so positive.

Those early childhood experiences with my parents piqued my curiosity about God and religion. They caused me to follow up with Bible study and to question friends and acquaintances who attended church more regularly than I. But I always ended up with more questions than answers, and the multitude of faiths practiced in my own small neighborhood often resulted in conflicting answers from different sources. It all seemed very confusing and complicated.

If I chose to study a single faith or denomination, I'd get only one perspective and miss all the others. How would I know which was right? On the other hand, if I pursued answers from every possible source, I would continue to be confused and wonder if any of it made sense. I wasn't trying to address deep theological questions. I was just a young kid who wanted to know if God was real, if He existed now or only in the past, and if He could hear and would answer my prayers.

I had other questions. Did God know who I was? Was He watching over my every move and protecting me? Were there really angels?

I also wondered a lot about Jesus and what it meant to be the Son of God. How could God be a single person and yet be in three forms?

When people said God spoke to them, were they lying or delusional? Did God really speak audibly? Why couldn't I hear God?

And why did so many bad things happen in the world—often to such good people? My list of questions seemed endless.

Simple questions like these eventually proved to be deeply theological after all. I didn't have good answers then and I don't have particularly good answers to all of them now, even after four years of divinity school studies. But during my lifetime, God's existence has been revealed to me and God has spoken to me. And as I read and reflect daily on Bible passages, I extract value and learn more about the nature, goodness, and grace of a loving, omnipresent God.

Sometimes my personal encounters with God have seemed coincidental, but I know they went far beyond coincidence; God was simply saying, "I'm real and I'm here for you." In other cases, God was admonishing me to recognize my own inappropriate behaviors and to change.

But the most pivotal episode of all happened when I was twelve. God's existence was revealed to me most dramatically through a mystical experience that occurred while I was contemplating the tough questions; I share that story in chapter 1. Not long thereafter, I came to recognize and accept Jesus Christ as my Lord and Savior. And from that moment on, I have never stopped believing.

I have not been alone in my seeking. My high school sweetheart and now wife, Sue, has remained my loving and faithful companion throughout this journey. We have shared the same questions and musings; both of us thirst to understand the meaning of life and the role of God and religion in our everyday existence.

Over the years, we have attended churches of various denominations. I never felt it necessary to attempt to identify the perfect theological match for my own beliefs because I never felt the nuances of differing

Christian denominations were really that important. What seemed most important to me was my conviction that God truly exists as the creator of the universe and that He is a living presence in the world today, just as He always has been and always will be.

My eagerness to speak to God, to pray for God's guidance, and to watch and listen for His response has grown throughout my lifetime. I have never heard God speak audibly and I have never seen Him in a vision, but I know God has been (and is) there. I know too that many of my experiences were not mere coincidence. God has indeed been speaking to me and revealing things I needed to know, to hear, and to act on.

If you are a Christian, what I have written is likely to reassure you that God is living and working in your life and that He delivers timely and critically important messages to you. I hope my words persuade you to be on the alert for such revelations—to remain vigilant and tuned in.

I hope reading about my life journey, coupled with reflection on your own, will cause you to contemplate the possibility that God was reaching out to you and sending you messages along the way.

I also hope it will make you ponder the things that have happened in your past so you will now recognize messages you may have initially missed.

Every life, including yours, is a journey that is important to God. As such, every life is one in which He will provide guidance, blessings, and unconditional love. I hope the words you are about to read will testify to that truth.

Chapter 1

GOD REVEALED . . .

IN
FAITH-STIRRING
EXPERIENCES

• •

As the chapter title suggests, the four stories that follow illustrate a few of the many events in my life when my faith was firmly established or reinforced by the palpable presence of God—in different ways, through different messengers. These were experiences where it was impossible to miss the significance of what was happening *when* it was happening. If you have had similar experiences, it is not likely you have forgotten them. But perhaps there is still more to learn from them by remembering.

I encourage you to read, remember, and reflect on how your life has been, or could have been, changed by those times when what was happening was incontrovertibly important. Realizations, even years later, may in fact be the key that unlocks the door to future enrichment.

My Mystical Adolescent Experience

At the age of twelve, I was a spiritual lightweight with heavy questions: Is God real? If He is, does He exist now or only in the past? Does God know who I am? Is He really watching over my every move? Will He answer my prayers? When people say God has spoken to them, are they lying or delusional? Does God really speak audibly, and if so, why can't I hear Him? And the list went on.

What little I had learned about God came from extended family, friends, and limited reading of the Bible. The fragments of the God story I'd gathered from these sources, as well as from differing Christian faith traditions and Jewish friends, did not present an intelligible or cohesive description of God; instead they elicited further questions.

It was a quiet, peaceful afternoon during my summer vacation from school in 1960. As an adolescent without a job, I found the summers provided ample time for baseball and thoughtful contemplation with little stress. My parents were working; my brother was down the street playing with friends; I was alone in a perfectly silent home. Lying on my bed with nothing to distract or interrupt me, my thoughts inevitably turned to the well-worn paths of my religious questioning.

What exactly would a world without beginning or end be? If God was eternal—existing before any physical matter or substance existed—who would be in this forever-world, even after the universe was no longer extant? I wasn't concerned about how all living things were created or how this created universe would ultimately end, but rather why humans were the superior intelligence and yet so inferior to God.

My mind was totally occupied with the possibility of an omniscient, omnipotent, and omnipresent God. I was not attempting to induce a mystical state, nor did I have any expectation of meeting God. I was simply engaged in deep contemplation over the questions and curiosities that consumed my young mind. While in this meditative state, however, I felt totally at peace—removed from the confines and constraints of my body. I could almost describe it as an "out-of-body" experience, although that description seems inadequate. I felt weightless, as if I were suspended above the floor of my room. I felt nothing but physical warmth, peace, quietude, painlessness, and great joy.

But these surreal sensations were dwarfed by something else: a very vivid connection with the Divine. No physical vision of God, no verbal communication, but an awareness of His presence that was unlike any I had ever felt before or have felt since. Enveloped and embraced by a bright warm light, I was filled with comfort and indescribable love. It was not unlike the comfort I often felt as a child just being in the presence of my parents, even when there was no physical embrace or verbal communication. Similarly, the pure, unconditional love I felt that day on my bed—of Divine parent for child—was reassuring and undeniable.

Oh, to remain in that state forever, but too quickly—in minutes— I felt myself drifting away from God's loving embrace. As the reality of my body and my physical surroundings crept back into my consciousness, I longed to go back, but sustaining the experience seemed out of my control.

A few days later, I had a brief reprise of this experience, but all future attempts to recreate it failed.

As I grew older, I repeatedly and futilely sought this transcendent experience. For years I feared I was drifting away from God because I couldn't return to the same feeling of closeness I had when I was twelve. Perhaps my mind had become cluttered with too many other interfering thoughts to be able to attain the same ecstatic, transcendent state.

The questions continued: Why had I been given this experience when I had no personal relationship with Jesus or any knowledge of saving grace? Had I experienced the love of the almighty God and was this God the same Jesus I had heard about? Were they really one and the same? What was this concept of the Trinity? Why would a young boy be given such a glimpse of God with no prior knowledge or context for the experience?

Despite my unanswered questions, I always recognized my experience as a gift from God, but I kept it to myself. As an adult, I worried that if I shared this event, others would consider me crazy or on the extreme religious fringe. But several years ago, I decided to risk it. It was at a retreat of the lay leadership of my church that I finally recounted my story. To my amazement, two other influential church leaders shared that they had enjoyed the exact same life-changing experience during their adolescence: During moments of meditation over similar questions, they had become aware of and felt close to God. And just like me, neither of them had been able to repeat this mystical state later in life.

Why had I been given this ecstatic glimpse of the Divine and why had it happened only twice? What was the point of what grew into a lifelong, seemingly futile, yearning to return? Could my yearning for such glory be part of God's plan for my life?

Once again, I was amazed to find that some answers would come from unexpected sharing—with a saint who lived almost two millennia ago. In my divinity school studies I wrote a research paper on Saint Augustine and read about two ascensions he had experienced more than 1,700 years ago that are documented in his famous *Confessions*. Like me, Augustine felt weighed down and rapidly pulled away from his mystical experiences, and, like me, he desperately wanted to return.

Augustine interpreted his ascensions as gifts from God and glimpses of the Divine; he determined that because of his own sinful nature, he was not able to repeat what had happened. As an adult, he had succumbed to temptation through carnal transgressions that he felt were the cause of this "weighed-down" feeling.

As an adolescent of only twelve years, I didn't have the same guilt over transgression, so I could not relate to this interpretation. However, in retrospect, I can accept that my human *capacity* to sin could separate me from the Divine.

As I read Augustine's accounts in this ancient text, I marveled at the similarities of our experiences . . . and a palpable sense that now finally—in my post-retirement studies—God was speaking directly to me through the recorded history of one of the great early Christian theologians.

Today I believe this kind of direct experience is a gift from God, a gift that instills a strong faith that enables the recipient to understand and follow God's divine calling. In my case, and in the case of my church colleagues, the calling was to become clergy or lay leaders in our faith communities. And perhaps our inability to reproduce the mystical state is also part of God's plan to create a burning desire to return to that ascension and to encourage others to seek a similar relationship with God.

Like Augustine, my church friends and I all came to realize in our evolving belief traditions that the way to achieve permanent salvation and assure ourselves of an ultimate ascension to God was through the saving grace of Jesus Christ. It could not be reproduced through future meditation or through replication of our adolescent events, but rather through accepting the sacrifice of Christ as our own redeeming grace.

My adolescent ascension convinced me that such mystical experiences are real and the accounts of theologians and others over the centuries are credible. I believe that my brief ascension to God was a gift that revealed aspects of the Divine I hadn't previously contemplated.

I am convinced that I did not trigger this ascension, but rather God willed it as a providential gift. God was not visible to me in an earthly sense but I came to "see" and "know" Him in a personal way and to believe unwaveringly in His existence. I can also now call it a gift of faith that ultimately led to my salvation through Christ and my permanent relationship with the Divine. To my delight, I learned that Augustine came to similar conclusions in his later writings.

I'm certain that many others over the centuries have enjoyed mystical experiences similar to my own. Fifty years after my own ascension and more than 1,700 years after Augustine's, the accounts in his Confessions spoke to me across the centuries to give me a better understanding of what happened to me and how it prepared me for, and indeed called me into, service in God's kingdom.

·············· *For Reflection* ···············

Yet I am always with you; you hold me by my right hand. You guide me with your counsel, and afterward you will take me into glory. Whom have I in heaven but you? And earth has nothing I desire besides you.

Psalm 73:23–25

···

I believe God provides experiences that reveal His existence, strengthen our faith, and give guidance. These revelations can occur not only when we are children, but at any time during our lives. At a crucial time of spiritual questioning, my experience undeniably confirmed to me that God was both real and aware of me. And even though I could not repeat the experience more than once, the faith-stirring impact has remained throughout my lifetime. I can joyfully echo the words of the Psalmist in proclaiming to God, "You hold me by my right hand," and with that knowledge, "earth has nothing I desire besides you."

Some of us are fortunate enough to recognize a divine presence at the time such a revelation occurs. Whether or not we immediately perceive His hand, however, these experiences allow us to develop greater faith and spirituality—even if we only learn from them in retrospect. If you're among those who never perceived a divine presence at the time of its occurrence, it may be very difficult now to identify such an experience, but I would still encourage you to try.

Think back on times when you were particularly distressed or challenged—perhaps when you brushed with danger, or when you felt moments of strong unconditional love from a parent, relative, or friend. Although at the time you may not have recognized the impact of a moment, you may find, looking back, that it was through God's presence in a single, fleeting moment that you came to believe that a higher power was possible, and even at work, in your life.

Almost every story in this book is a retrospective reaffirmation of God's active role in guiding and shaping my spiritual awareness and development. I find it ironic—and yet hopeful—that I'm learning from some of these experiences only now. Perhaps this delayed learning—lessons to be unwrapped at future moments in our lives—is also part of His spiritual tutoring and plan for us. The passage of time often has a way of "sharpening" the lens through which we view these moments as they really were—revelations of His existence.

Sue's Prayers

During my early years of marriage, I was obsessively driven to succeed in my career. And ironically what helped keep Sue and me together was her response to my nearly all-consuming work-related efforts; she was not only tolerant, but she was supportive of my work habits and time away from the family.

I knew I was neglecting my family as a father and as a husband. Because of the heavy work demands, I typically slept only four or five hours a night for almost thirty years—certainly not a healthy habit.

In an attempt to manage my time more effectively, and create family experiences and personal interactions with Sue and the kids, I adopted a few coping techniques that helped. I took annual one-on-one trips with each of the five kids, we would take at least one full family vacation every year, and I practiced liberal use of email correspondence and daily prayer.

Involvement in the church helped as well. Early in our marriage, Sue and I began to regularly attend church, Sunday school classes, and church-related events. We also served the Lord in leadership roles within the church community. Sue taught Sunday school and church-sponsored day care while I served as a deacon or trustee in many of the churches we attended. These practices added a welcomed faith-related dimension to our lives that most certainly enabled us to better cope with the otherwise hectic pace. But in a strange way it also added to our stress by consuming even more of the precious limited number of hours available each day.

My various coping techniques provided some relief from stress, but there is one profoundly dramatic factor that has had the greatest impact on our relationship—a factor that came by way of Sue's grandmother.

Sue's paternal grandmother, Grace Smolar, was a woman I loved deeply and respected greatly for her expressions of faith to her family members. She prayed before every meal and taught Sue to say bedtime prayers every night. And it was this practice that contributed to the strength of our marriage, especially one night during one of our most tumultuous early years.

I was a young executive attempting to climb the corporate ladder, but despite working very long hours and devoting myself entirely to my career, I was losing favor with an extremely demanding boss who wasn't satisfied with anything less than superhuman results. I worried about losing my job. At the same time, my father had been diagnosed with cancer and I had little time to devote to him or to my young family. The stress was affecting me physically. I'd dropped from my normal 200 pounds to 170 and my typically healthy, smiling face reflected sadness and sleep deprivation.

I was dead tired but so stressed over my future, our finances, my seeming inability to "get it all done," that my body simply would not relax. Much as I longed for sleep, it would not come. But after what seemed like hours, finally exhaustion overcame me, and just as I felt myself about to drift off, I heard Sue:

"Dear God, please be with Fred and give him the strength and courage to deal with the difficult situation at work, help him to reconcile his differences and misunderstandings with his boss," she whispered in that lovely, soft, voice. "God, please relieve Fred's stress so that he may regain his strength and his health while he also frees up time to spend with his ailing father and his children. They miss him and need him, Lord." Sue was saying her nightly prayers.

She probably thought I was finally out and couldn't hear her words—but I did hear them, and so did God. Tears welled up in my eyes and a lump filled my throat as I tried to avoid audibly sobbing—interrupting her prayers and revealing that I was listening to her intimate conversation.

How many times over the years this happened. And how precious these moments are to me. This is what got us through the rough spots: knowing that I was not alone, that my spouse was a strong believer, and that she was not simply relying on me to see us through the challenges of young married life.

Today I am convinced that God indeed listened to and answered Sue's—and my—prayers. I thank God daily for faithful grandmothers, mothers, and spouses. They are some of the principal people who have made such an important contribution to my faith, my spiritual development, and my happiness. And their influence, passed on to my wife, has been a key factor in the strength of our marriage.

.... *For Reflection* ....

And the prayer offered in faith will make the sick person well; the Lord will raise them up. If they have sinned, they will be forgiven. Therefore confess your sins to each other and pray for each other so that you may be healed. The prayer of a righteous person is powerful and effective.

James 5:15–16

God has spoken to me through the voice of my wife, Sue, on many occasions. She has been an incredibly supportive wife of a certifiable workaholic while she very ably ran the household and raised five children. Witnessing and hearing her bedtime prayers touched me greatly and led me to a far deeper relationship with God. While she was speaking intently and sincerely to God, He was speaking to me through her.

Think back on how you have come to your own Christian faith. My guess is there have been pillars of faith in your background who set an example for you and whose abiding faith was an inspiration in your own spiritual development. Try to recall who they were, what they did or said to influence you, and how you might uplift others.

As indicated in James 5, Sue's prayers offered in abiding faith helped to cure my "sickness" and relieve my stress. By confessing your sins, praying for each other, and revealing your faith, you can become a blessing to others, not only in your immediate household but also among all of your friends and acquaintances. Let your faith be known to your family first but also to those in your circle of friends and colleagues, and pray for one another. God will not only richly reward you for doing so but will impact others through you as He impacted me through Sue.

Saving a Family from Ruin

As a high-ranking executive in the life insurance industry, I was pretty far removed from the customer. I spent much more of my time interacting with agents and employees than with our customers. The most important and direct interactions that the company had with customers happened through the life insurance agent, who would initially make the sale, help to service the account, and then ultimately submit the death claim for a grieving family.

For agents, making the sale is perhaps their most challenging task. A life insurance contract is an intangible product that essentially represents a promise to pay claims in the future after the death of the insured life. Many people resist making a significant purchase for which the only perceived return is a payment to their beneficiaries from an insurance company after their death. A relatively high percentage of men and women who enter the life insurance business as agents fail because they simply can't convince people to make that initial purchase. In response to this particular challenge unique to the insurance industry, the industry has developed a number of ways to encourage sales personnel and reward hard-won sales records. One such incentive is qualification for membership in the Million Dollar Round Table (MDRT). Begun in 1927, MDRT is an independent, international association of tens of thousands of sales professionals in the life insurance and financial services industries who are recognized for their excellence in professional performance, ethical conduct, and client service.

In 1998, I attended the MDRT annual meeting, a huge industry gathering, which was held that year at a large convention center in Chicago. A staggering 7,000 people were in attendance. I was there as an honored guest, but most attendees were insurance agents who had qualified to attend based on their high level of annual sales. The MDRT consisted of platform presentations to the full group of delegates every morning and smaller breakout sessions conducted each afternoon. The morning platform sessions were well known for their emotional content, and attendees always came prepared to be moved by what they heard.

One of those main platform presentations was by David Woods, CEO of an industry association that publicized the importance of life insurance in protecting the financial future of families who lose the primary income earner. David showed a very moving, professionally produced video about a young family with two small children who had lost their father in an automobile accident. He had been killed only two days after purchasing a life insurance policy.

The young widow talked about her husband, and the children spoke emotionally about their dad. The widow said that her husband's life insurance had saved them from financial ruin, allowing them to maintain their home and lifestyle and even provide for the kids' education. There wasn't a dry eye in the house. Indeed, the short video segment reassured the large audience of insurance professionals that our life's work is significant and that it provides great value to consumers—consumers who don't always recognize the devastating risks they face and who often object to "wasting money" on life insurance.

But the tears streaming down my face were for a very different, private reason. You see, I knew the rest of the story. In an audience of 7,000 people representing more than 200 insurance companies, God was speaking directly to *me*.

As I'd watched the video, the family's situation sounded strangely familiar. But it wasn't until the family's agent was interviewed at the end of the video that I made the connection. I was certain this case had come across my desk at New York Life several months earlier.

As president of the company, I rarely had to make decisions on death claims. Those decisions were almost always handled by executives at a lower level in the corporate hierarchy. But this one had come to me from the legal department. They felt we were not obligated to pay the family's claim because their application had not been submitted with an initial premium payment. Therefore, on the date of the father's sudden death, state insurance laws mandated that his life insurance coverage was not technically in effect and enforceable through the insurance company.

Our company lawyers recommended I deny the claim. They felt that if I paid the claim, I would potentially set a legal precedent that was beyond our technical contractual liability.

However, there was one extenuating circumstance: The father who lost his life in that car accident had written and signed a check for the premium payment to New York Life Insurance Company. The check was sitting on his desk at home the day he was killed.

When I reviewed the situation, I didn't have time to read the entire file. I didn't know about the wife and kids; for me, this was nothing more than a business decision. I thought about the financial loss to the company if we were to pay the claim. I also thought briefly about the precedent I might be setting by approving it. I knew other agents could potentially demand similar treatment, even when similar extenuating circumstances did not exist. Nonetheless, given the evidence, I decided that the "right thing to do" was to pay the claim. I signed the claim and went on with my work as always. I didn't think about the situation again—that is, until Chicago.

Seeing the video at that time was not mere coincidence. Hundreds of companies were represented at this convention; thousands of agents from around the world were in this audience; and this one video told of one family that had insurance coverage with just one company. The outcome hinged on one executive who made a difficult decision that would forever impact the family's financial future. That executive was *me*. And I was the only one who knew it.

Here's the miracle: At the time of the Chicago meeting, I was questioning the value of what I did for a living. I frequently bemoaned the sacrifices I was making in my own family life to take on such a huge vocational responsibility. As the video ended, it was suddenly crystal clear to me: God had chosen this venue, this story, to reassure me. God was making me aware of the importance of what I did for a living. Just as importantly, God was emphasizing the importance of integrity—of doing what was "right" instead of relying on legal loopholes and technicalities.

Needless to say, this experience with its resulting epiphany changed me forever. It not only changed the way I conducted business, but also how I lived my life. I subsequently told the story to thousands of agents and employees at New York Life, which gave me an opportunity both to express my faith and to indicate the importance of the work our agents and employees did to provide important benefits to our customers when they need it the most. Sharing my experience also helped motivate agents who were typically reluctant to approach prospective clients with a proposal to buy life insurance—a motivator for the agents and a potentially great blessing for their clients.

But the greatest change for me came in knowing I needed to be more attuned to, and listen more carefully for, messages from God. His message was one I desperately needed to hear, and as He always does, He found the perfect way to deliver it.

················ *For Reflection* ···············

You have searched me, Lord, and you know me.
You know when I sit and when I rise;
you perceive my thoughts from afar.
You discern my going out and my lying down;
you are familiar with all my ways.
Before a word is on my tongue you,
Lord, know it completely.
You hem me in behind and before,
and you lay your hand upon me.
Such knowledge is too wonderful for me,
too lofty for me to attain.
Where can I go from your spirit?
Where can I flee from your presence?
If I go up to the heavens, you are there;
if I make my bed in the depths, you are there.
If I rise on the wings of the dawn,

if I settle on the far side of the sea,
even there your hand will guide me,
your right hand will hold me fast.

Psalm 139:1–10

. . . .

The experience in Chicago was one of the most moving of my life. It came at a time when I needed vocational reassurances. It not only reinforced my faith, but it also reminded me of the profound value of my profession and the efforts of insurance industry sales representatives and employees. Sitting in an audience of 7,000 people, I palpably felt God's presence. I had no doubt that God was speaking directly to me, as I was the only person in the massive audience who knew the "rest of the story."

Certainly there have been many times in your life when you struggled with tough decisions or you questioned your purpose. We all face those moments. And it is equally certain that there will be many more moments like that in your future. As you reach out to God for guidance, take comfort in knowing as the Psalmist wrote, "Before a word is on my tongue you, Lord, know it completely." If your answers to prayer and messages from God are like mine, you probably won't audibly hear God. So you need to be tuned in for His nonverbal communications. Watch for those highly improbable but well-timed experiences that prove to be providential and not coincidental. It just may be His hand guiding you and holding you fast.

Epiphany in India

Between 2002 and 2007, I made fifteen trips to India for New York Life. Those trips were necessary due to a partnership we had established with MaxIndia, a highly respected health-care company that owned clinics and hospitals throughout India. MaxIndia did everything possible to help maintain a good relationship with us, even though we were allowed only a twenty-four percent ownership interest in the partnership and didn't have a voting majority on the governing board. Despite the management challenges, frequent visits allowed us to successfully oversee the company remotely.

Initially, I had concerns about traveling so frequently to such a distant land with such a different regulatory, legal, and cultural environment. I had also heard stories about infrastructure problems, poor water quality, and extensive and pervasive poverty, all of which added to my concerns. It wasn't long before I saw that everything I had heard was true.

But despite the multitude of serious issues besetting the country, India's economy was booming, the financial services industry was thriving, and New York Life's growth in life insurance sales was astounding. In the first five or six years of operation in the country, we more than doubled new sales each year and our staff had grown from a handful of people to more than 10,000 agents and employees. This was one of our greatest global success stories and I was pleased to be an important part of it.

I also grew to love India and its ambitious and industrious people, but it took several visits before I could fully appreciate the vibrancy of the culture, the people, and the rapidly expanding economy. I never fully adjusted to the highly visible and unavoidable signs of abject poverty in both the urban and rural areas. The only exception seemed to be the most affluent communities in the larger cities, but even there I was never more than a few minutes from the less fortunate majority of the population. I was pleased that New York Life felt a social obligation to contribute to various charitable causes in the country, and on many of my visits I was delighted to present checks to local adoption agencies and other worthy nonprofit organizations. I prayed often for the people of India and looked forward to each trip there, realizing that through this business arrangement I had found a way to express my faith and to do God's work.

After one of our board meetings, MaxIndia Chairman Analjit Singh invited me to visit the newest and most technologically advanced cardiac hospital in New Delhi. As we walked into the attractive and modern atrium of the hospital entrance, Analjit asked if I wanted to observe a surgical procedure. At first I was reluctant; I wasn't sure how I might react to the sight of blood during open-heart surgery. However, I suspected I'd be observing from a surgical amphitheater at least ten or twelve feet above the operating table, and I figured I could easily step back or look away if I felt the least bit uneasy. Moreover, I was excited by the prospect of witnessing something few people ever have a chance to observe. So with my amphitheater-facilitated escape mechanism in mind, I enthusiastically agreed.

After a brief tour of the facility and an interesting meeting with the hospital's chief of staff and one of its most prominent surgeons, I was taken into a pre-surgery scrub room. There, along with doctors preparing for surgery, I was asked to remove all of my clothing, to scrub my hands and arms, and to don a surgical gown, mask, hat, and booties. These were not precautions that would be required for viewing from an amphitheater! My heart raced; my blood pressure soared. However, I also was a bit disappointed: no doubt the view of the procedure from a poorly positioned location in the operating room would be inferior to what I'd see from an elevated position in the amphitheater.

After scrubbing and dressing, I was shown into an operating room where a quadruple bypass surgery was already in progress. To my shock and surprise, the hospital official who escorted me into the room asked the anesthesiologist who stood at the head of the operating table to step aside so I could stand right next to the table. What happened next was profoundly moving.

As I nervously approached and stood between the cardiac monitoring devices by the patient's head, I had a fleeting thought about legal liability and how a nonmedical visitor in the United States would never be allowed to get this close to an active surgical procedure. My stomach was literally no more than two inches from the top of the patient's head, and I was very conscious of avoiding any contact with him or the monitoring devices. I clasped my hands behind my back and held them tightly together for fear that I might touch something I wasn't supposed to touch.

On my right stood the chief surgeon and an assistant surgeon, and on my left, the chief surgical nurse and an assistant surgical nurse. The anesthesiologist was right behind me watching the cardiac monitors. She had moved to make room for me, and no one else noticed or acknowledged my presence as they worked methodically on the patient.

Having taken a moment to get my bearings after inserting myself into this unique and somewhat uncomfortable environment, I finally glanced at the patient's open chest cavity to observe, directly in front of me and no more than eighteen inches from my nose, a regularly and methodically beating heart on which the surgeons were sewing the final few sutures. I stared in amazement, totally engrossed and enthralled.

My heart rate soared as I observed the beating heart in front of me. What a marvel of medical science that such a surgery was possible. Who first thought he could cut open a chest cavity and tamper with the human heart without killing the patient in the process? What skill it took and what daring to perform such a surgery for the first time. How many patients were lost in the process of educating and developing these skilled practitioners? And then I thought how the litigious environment in the United States was probably stifling the advancement of medical science by creating deterrents to experimentation with innovative new procedures and techniques.

However, my most moving and enduring reaction to this wonderful experience was a profoundly spiritual one—one I had clearly not expected when I first nervously entered the operating room.

Standing next to the patient, I suddenly realized that I was not nearly as amazed by the work of the surgeons and the advancement of medical science as I was by God's creation.

In front of me, a fully exposed human heart beat continuously and regularly for twenty or thirty minutes without missing a thump while surgeons confidently finished their work. Even an unhealthy heart could beat continuously for seventy or eighty years, or even longer. The heart never takes a break, not even when we're sleeping. I began to weep as I suddenly realized that for me this experience was not about technology or the advancement of medical science in India—this was about creation. God's creation.

What makes that happen? What is the underlying source of life? And how can anyone deny the existence of a divine creator?

As I watched the heart before me, I knew this could not possibly happen by chance. We have yet to find even a single-cell form of life on any other planet, yet the earth is teaming with life. There are more living cells in a teaspoon of our pond water or soil than there are in the rest of the known universe. And here on this operating table was the highest form of life: a man with many highly complex organs, only one of which I was observing. There are so many other marvelous aspects to creation in both the animal and plant kingdoms, and for this one moment in India, I was given a close look at perhaps the most marvelous of all God's created life forms and its life-sustaining engine: the human heart.

There have been several moments in my life when I very palpably felt the presence of God; this was one of them. During such moments, I often cried with joy, and this was no exception. I fought back the tears out of concern that they might run down my cheeks and drip onto the patient's head. Fortunately, my soft cotton surgical mask absorbed the tears that couldn't be suppressed. In that fleeting but memorable moment, I realized how God was vividly revealing to me the wonder of creation. As a businessman originally trained in mathematics and probability, it is much harder for me to believe that somehow humans randomly evolved from an amoeba than it is to believe that this was God's handiwork and grand design.

God opened my eyes and my mind and renewed my faith when I saw Him and His glorious creation reflected by a human heart that day in New Delhi, India. It's an experience that has changed my perspective on life forever.

·············· *For Reflection* ···············

For since the creation of the world God's invisible qualities— his eternal power and divine nature—have been clearly seen, being understood from what has been made, so that men are without excuse. For although they knew God, they neither glorified Him as God, nor gave thanks to Him, but their thinking became futile and their foolish hearts were darkened.

Romans 1:20–22

···

On that memorable visit to India, the wonder of God's marvelous creation was revealed to me in a way that profoundly impacted my faith. It occurred in a setting I never could have imagined myself in—a sophisticated cardiac facility that I never would have believed existed amid the poverty and deprivation around me.

In my many years on this planet, how often I have missed the opportunity to marvel at the wonder of God's creation in the cosmos, in plants, in animals, and in human creation. What a shame that I have toiled through my daily life without reflecting on or even recognizing God's creation and the intricacies and beauty of my existence and the things I am privileged to experience through my five senses.

Every person reading these words has multiple opportunities daily to briefly stop what they're doing and catch a glimpse of God and His creation. What in nature, within your eyesight right now, exists anywhere else in the known universe? Do you believe it all came about by chance? Do you not marvel at the wonder of what God has made? Can you relate to Paul's admonition to the Romans that foolish hearts can be darkened to the realities of God's existence and divine creation? I certainly can! Paul says we have no excuse to miss it, but so many of us do!

I have known several people who have recovered from life-threatening accidents or illnesses who are eager to share how they now live life and perceive their surroundings differently. They now more fully appreciate and acknowledge God's creation. Don't wait for a near-death experience to receive that joy and to share it with others. Paul, in his letter to the Romans, warns about the foolishness of those who don't recognize the undeniable existence of God as revealed in creation.

Chapter 1 Exercises

Chapter 1 revealed experiences in which I very tangibly felt God's presence and influence. These were faith-stirring experiences that will be etched in my memory forever, serving as a constant reminder of when and how my faith was originally established and later fortified.

In God's Presence

Not everyone experiences the kind of glorious connection to God that I did at age twelve, as described in the story "My Mystical Adolescent Experience." But can you recall an experience in your own youth when you first felt close to God and began to believe in His existence?

- Briefly describe that experience and how you felt at the time.
- Are you more or less certain now than you were then that the experience was providential? Why?
- With whom, and how, can you comfortably share that experience in a way that will make a positive impact?

Pillars of Faith

When I think back on people in my life who represented pillars of faith—people I greatly admired, people who significantly influenced my own faith—I think first of my wife's grandmother, Grace Smolar.

- Is there someone in your life whom you recognize as a pillar of faith?
- Who was that person and in what ways were you able to observe his or her faithfulness?
- Describe how your memories of that person continue to impact you.
- When do you find yourself thinking of him or her?
- What are the ways in which you might become that pillar of faith to others in the future?

Divine Marvels

In the story "Epiphany in India," I palpably felt God's influence and presence as I observed His incredible human creation. Some people have told me they see God's handiwork in the vastness and harmony of the cosmos, while others say they marvel at the complexity and intricacy of microscopic particles and life forms.

- What are some of the most faith-stirring experiences you've had as you live daily and observe God's creation?
- As you discuss answers to this question with others, consider whether or not you have overlooked or taken for granted the wonders of your daily surroundings. What have you missed?
- In your daily life, are you using all of your senses to experience the wonder of God's creation?
- Are there ways that you can find to share your renewed wonder at God's creation with others?

Chapter 2

GOD REVEALED . . .

THROUGH OUR FRIENDSHIPS

P eople are often reluctant to tell their stories for fear of rendering themselves transparent or even vulnerable. But the voices of friends can represent and deliver messages God wants us to hear, teaching or revealing deep truths or lessons that we might otherwise not benefit from or experience directly. If you have missed such messages delivered through friends in the past, chances are this is a fruitful area to revisit for evidence of God speaking to you.

As you read the following stories of God speaking to me through my friends, there may be lessons I learned that are applicable to you as well. But more importantly, think back on your own interactions with friends. Perhaps a friend revealed issues in his or her life that you found strangely similar to your own. Perhaps you learned or could have learned something from that conversation and just maybe God was sending you a message. I encourage you to think of how you may have benefitted in the intervening years if you had only listened, heard, and acted on those messages. It may not be too late.

My Friend Warren

After graduating from Amherst College in 1970, I moved back to Michigan to pursue a teaching career only to find a market glutted with teachers, primarily because the Vietnam War offered a draft deferral for teachers. The application process was extraordinarily frustrating and demoralizing, with hundreds of applicants for every position; just getting an interview was a major success, and securing a job seemed impossible. Though I would have preferred to teach high school mathematics, the competition for those positions was greatest. The best I could get was an entry-level position teaching largely remedial mathematics at Franklin Junior High School in the Wayne-Westland School District.

Although it was less intellectually challenging to teach mathematics at the junior high school level, the younger students were far more impressionable and in greater need of positive role models than were high school students. As a result, I felt I was doing noble work and changing the world in my own small way—not only teaching, but coaching football, wrestling, and track. I sensed I was doing the work God intended me to do.

Eventually I moved into more advanced math courses and also taught a beginning-level course in photography, which I pursued as an avocation. Not only was this something I loved, but teaching photography allowed me to spend each morning preparing for class in the darkroom in the school's science wing. It was there that I met and became close friends with a number of science teachers—among them Warren Rysberg, who became my best friend among the faculty.

Warren had a zest for life, an amazing sense of humor, and a presence and charisma greater than almost anyone I had ever known. He loved his work, loved his students, and loved his fellow faculty members. We soaked up each other's company and loved sharing our classroom experiences and our successes as well as our failures in impacting students' lives.

And we were tested. There was no greater satisfaction than realizing I had touched a student on meaningful levels and helped change his or her life, but few frustrations compared to the inability to touch certain students, a situation that could be very depressing.

Despite my respect, appreciation, and affection for my teaching colleagues—especially Warren—after teaching in Wayne-Westland for six years, I could no longer live with the uncertainty of getting layoff slips in the spring and not knowing until summer whether my contract would be renewed in the fall, so in the summer of 1977, I decided to move on. Given my strong mathematics background, I wanted to try my hand at the actuarial profession, and my young family and I went to Boston.

It was a decision I would never regret, but as often happens with long-distance relocations, I lost touch with my former friends. Communication became less frequent; eventually some holiday greeting cards didn't reach intended recipients, whose addresses had changed. Sadly, even my important friendship with Warren went into suspended animation.

Many years later, long after Warren and I had last made contact, another dear friend, science teacher Sue Johnson, did a Google search of my name and discovered that I was working at New York Life Insurance Company.

"Warren has cancer," she told me over the phone. "He's not doing particularly well; he's retired." She gave me his new address and phone number and said she was sure he would enjoy hearing from me.

Surprised by the strength of my feelings after such a long time with no contact, I called Warren immediately. His voice, too, surprised me. Not only was he in excellent spirits, but he was genuinely excited to hear from me. As if no time had passed, we resumed our easy conversation, catching up on what had transpired over the years, reminiscing about old times at Franklin with some of the more colorful students and teachers from that era. He also updated me on the whereabouts of numerous other friends from the school.

"Let's stay in touch," he said, laughing that old familiar effervescent laugh.

"I will," I promised. "Warren, I want you to know I'll be praying for you—for your recovery." His cancer was late stage.

"Thanks, Fred. I appreciate it."

Warren and I did stay in touch, and in the process, I connected not only with Sue Johnson but also with Barb Duncan, another dear friend from my teaching days.

In the many emails, calls, and cards we exchanged over the following couple of years, I started to talk to Sue and Barb about the two of them visiting the New York area with Warren. He had always wanted to travel to New York City; in particular, he wanted to go to Ellis Island to see if he could track down records of some of his ancestors who had entered the country there in the early twentieth century.

My wife, Sue, and I offered to have the three of them stay at our home in Connecticut, and plans were successfully pieced together for a five-day visit in May 2005. Initially I was very excited about the chance to spend time with my former friends, but as the day of their arrival drew closer, I began to get apprehensive—it had been more than twenty-five years. Would we have enough to talk about after such a long time? And what about Warren's condition? Would it restrict his ability to get around? And given my job responsibilities, could I really take enough time from work to give our visitors adequate attention without causing major work disruptions?

From the moment the group arrived until the sad moment when they departed, the experience was a reunion of friends that was absolutely glorious and a timely blessing from God. Warren was his normal, ebullient self; had it not been for the chemotherapy-induced hair loss, I would not have been able to tell he was ill. His positive attitude, his appreciation for our friendship, and his gusto for living were remarkable and inspiring. We laughed uncontrollably over events I'd nearly forgotten. My children and my mother-in-law became quite enamored with my three long-time friends.

One day we took a private guided tour of New York City with an eccentric but fascinating city historian, author, and guide named Timothy "Speed" Levitch. Speed was a city dweller who spoke of the sights and sounds of New York City in grand metaphorical and poetic terms, while

Warren's down-home, country-boy background gave him a far different reaction to the busy city streets. The banter and contrast between the two of them had us all in stitches.

Thanks to Sue Johnson's preplanning, we had front-row center seats for *The Lion King*, giving our visitors from Michigan a bird's-eye view of the orchestra pit from directly behind the conductor. Oh, the joy and wonder on my friends' faces as they watched a very popular first-class Broadway production from a front-row perspective. I found myself watching them as much as I was watching the play. What an amazing and rare friendship and history we had. Why had I let my career ambitions, my busyness, and the geographical distances separate me from these dear friends for so long?

The next day we took the ferry ride to both the Statue of Liberty and Ellis Island, where we walked the grounds, perused the shops, and asked about Warren's ancestors at the Ellis Island site—allowing Warren to finally fulfill the original intent of his visit to New York.

In the sweetness of our arm-in-arm walk to the Statue of Liberty, I also felt the impending loss. I'd finally reconnected with my friend, and now he would leave me. And I thought about my own mortality and how I'd one day be saying my own good-byes. With my whole heart, I suddenly felt the value and great joy of true friendship and how the power and purity of God's love can find expression in such relationships.

Our time together and the events we chose to share proved to be a fitting reunion of four long-time friends and associates. But most meaningful for me were the times during the five-day visit when Warren and I had a chance to be together privately.

How do you describe the value of silence? Communion? Perhaps that's what I experienced with Warren as we simply sat in rich silence and just enjoyed each other's presence while thinking of the past, absorbing the present, and contemplating the future.

We did speak about his illness and his prognosis. But that too was touched by silence. "Warren," I assured him, "you are immortal. I'm sure of it. I know it through my faith; I truly believe in a glorious afterlife."

Warren didn't say a lot, but he later shared with me and others how important those reassurances were and how he derived such hope from my expressed certainty.

On several other occasions during the visit, Warren advised me with similar certainty. "Fred," he said, "you have got to stop and smell the roses. Why don't you at least consider retiring early so you can spend more time with Sue and the kids? You need time to follow your passions while you're still here."

I shared with him my plans to retire early to attend divinity school, teach, and write.

"I love it!" he responded. "Do it! Do it without doubt or hesitation. You won't regret it."

We reminisced, we hugged, and we shared mutual respect and admiration during those five short days—days that will remain etched in my mind forever—and I dreaded saying good-bye.

The day of their departure, I had to leave very early to go to my office in New York City, so I woke at 4 a.m. to write Warren a note:

Warren:

I can't tell you how much this weekend has meant to me. Seeing you again and enjoying time together laughing and reminiscing has been truly special for me and really very therapeutic. My own illness (workaholism) is in many ways more devastating and fatal than your cancer.

You have been one of my very best friends and I only regret that I let so many years get away with such little direct contact. I thank God that He allowed me the true privilege and honor of seeing you again with Barb and Sue over such a glorious week together.

You have touched so many lives in so many ways that none of us can ever dream of living a more full and complete life.

I have been praying for you every day since I heard of your illness, and I will continue to do so. I knew immediately when I saw you that God had answered those prayers because you looked so terrific and full of "life." Clearly God is not done with you yet and I'm certain God will give you more time to spread your wonderful humor, love, and joy to all of those whom you continue to touch.

Thank you for reminding me what life is really all about before it was too late for me.

Your friend forever,

Fred

I maintained fairly frequent contact by phone with Warren after that visit in 2005. He had no children and his wife, Wanda, was confined to a nursing home, so for the next many months Sue Johnson often visited Warren at his home in the Upper Peninsula of Michigan, helping him sort out his affairs and prepare for his death. She also kept me informed of his condition, so I knew when the end was near.

In mid-June of 2006, I called Warren. He was weak and heavily medicated, but his spirits remained high. Sue was with him and put him on the phone.

"I love you, Warren," I told him. "I love you and I owe you. You were instrumental in my decision to retire at fifty-nine and attend Yale Divinity School. 'Make the choice quickly,' you said. 'Implement it without doubt or hesitation.' I've done it, my friend, and I can't thank you enough for your trust in the strength of our friendship and for pushing me so hard."

He was quiet, but he seemed pleased.

Then, with tears streaming down my face and a painful lump in my throat, I said my final words: "Warren, I love you and I'll see you on the other side."

Warren passed away two or three days later, and I, along with hundreds of others, attended his funeral in Michigan—a celebration of the life of a remarkable man. Warren Rysberg hadn't been the leader of a large company or even the head of the small science department at Franklin Junior High School, but through his career and over the course of his life he touched the lives of thousands.

··············· *For Reflection* ···············

Be devoted to one another in brotherly love. Honor one another above yourselves. Never be lacking in zeal, but keep your spiritual fervor, serving the Lord. Be joyful in hope, patient in affliction, faithful in prayer.

Romans 12:10–12

·· ·········

Our life's journey is sharply defined by the collection of people we encounter—especially those we ultimately consider close friends—who reflect God's love through their loyal, supportive, and enduring friendship. Unfortunately, in today's fast-paced mobile society we often change jobs, relocate, and lose touch with those dearest to us. After more than twenty-five years of separation from Warren, God brought us back together in a way I never could have predicted that positively impacted both of our lives.

My reunion with Warren came at a time when I was intently focused on the pursuit of my career at New York Life. Warren's illness and his encouragement to retire and follow other passions were instrumental in the critical decisions I would make and execute in the subsequent two years. God most certainly brought us together again and delivered an important message to me through Warren's voice.

In the busyness of our lives, how easy it is for us to lose track of former close friends. Are there people in your life with whom you wish you could reconnect and see again? The people search capability of the Internet provides us with the opportunity to almost instantly relocate long-lost friends. I encourage you to find those special friends in your life with whom you have lost touch.

In your renewal of old friendships, you may be blessed as I was in my reunion with Warren. And as Paul suggested in his letter to the Romans, it may not be too late to devote yourself to one another and express your joy in hope, your patience in affliction, or your faithfulness in prayer.

Finding Your Greatness

In the mid-2000s I was trying to decide what passions to pursue in my retirement years. Over the course of my career, I'd had several diverse work experiences and had seriously committed to following my passions in multiple areas.

In the early 1970s, after receiving a bachelor's degree from Amherst College, I taught junior high school and simultaneously earned a master's degree in mathematics at Wayne State University (WSU) in Detroit.

And now, thirty years later, as I approached the final chapter of my career at New York Life Insurance Company, once again I was trying to figure out what I was meant to do. It was during this time that WSU President Irvin Reid took me and my wife, Sue, to dinner and the opera in New York City. It was a lovely evening, during which we discussed many of WSU's educational and community initiatives in and around Detroit—both those that were underway as well as those planned for the future. The school's long-term strategic plan was especially impressive; it included significant new building on campus, increased scholarship programs, expanded research, and much greater outreach to the Detroit community. Given my interest in and experience teaching mathematics, I was particularly fascinated by WSU's already-successful teaching program for students in the public school system. They call it the "Math Corps."

The Math Corps was started more than twenty years ago by two WSU math professors, Steve Kahn and Leonard Boehm, and involves students from fifth through twelfth grade. The program is not designed to cater to the gifted; rather, it involves ordinary (by most standards "remedial") students who can ultimately earn college credit for calculus proficiency while still in high school. It has had a particularly strong success rate in providing high-quality educational support to inner-city kids, who historically have scored poorly on standardized math tests.

The Math Corps also conducts a summer program for more than 200 students and hires seventy teachers who have been trained by Steve and Leonard. Many of these teachers are former students of the Math Corps who have gone on to earn college degrees and are now entering the teaching field. (Many other graduates have pursued careers in mathematics and other math-related professions.)

The program is similar to the teaching in the movie *Stand and Deliver*—the true story of an innovative and dedicated math teacher in the inner-city schools of Los Angeles who taught calculus to groups of high school students. These students achieved unprecedented pass rates on advanced-placement calculus tests and received college credit for first-year calculus. In fact, the pass rates were so high that the students were falsely accused of cheating.

According to WSU President Irvin Reid, those were the kind of results achieved by the Math Corps in Detroit. Little did I know as we talked about the program that evening in New York City that I would actually get to see it in action—not once, but twice—with very unexpected results.

The first time I saw the program in action was six or seven years ago when Sue and I attended an inner-city class taught by Leonard Boehm at Thurgood Marshall Elementary School. Only three weeks into the school year, these fifth-grade students were excited, engaged, and extremely responsive to Leonard's teaching style. They participated enthusiastically and were treated very respectfully by Leonard and their fellow classmates. The material was difficult and how quickly they mastered it! Watching Leonard in action stirred up my old passion for teaching. Here in this underprivileged neighborhood among these ordinary students, a truly gifted man was having a long-term impact. This man was doing what he was meant to do.

And how about me? Was I using my gifts adequately? Was I contributing to long-term impact and adding value in a meaningful way?

While I've donated financially to this worthy effort over the years, it wasn't until the summer of 2009 that I had my second opportunity to see why the Math Corps is so successful and what message God was sending, through that success, to me.

It was a hot Saturday afternoon in July when I asked Steve and Leonard to join me at a Detroit Tigers baseball game. Leonard couldn't make it because of a family emergency, but Steve came with his two adopted children. Sue and I adopted three children and, like Steve, loved to involve them in leisure activities, so I immediately established a rapport with him.

I couldn't tell you what happened on the baseball diamond that afternoon. Nor was there talk of mathematics. The message came from somewhere else entirely.

"You know how I got to know who I am?" asked Steve.

"No," I answered, wondering where this was going.

"Twenty-five years ago, when I volunteered to teach math to a group of the toughest inner-city kids in the Detroit School District, I didn't have a clue. I was nervous. After all, these were kids who had been expelled from their regular school and sent to a detention-like special facility for disturbed and delinquent students. It was a seemingly impossible task for a new teacher, but it was in the process of confronting that challenge head-on that I discovered my own gifts."

As I listened openmouthed, Steve recounted his unwavering belief—even as a young teacher—that "every human being on the planet has inherent greatness." After talking about the kids, he shared other examples: Steve's father, a beloved clothing store owner in Brooklyn, had such a tremendous impact on his community that following his death, he was honored by a farewell parade down Gerritson Avenue. Then there was the story of Stephen Holder, a former remedial math student with no parents who was struggling to raise his siblings on his own—and who went on to earn a master's degree in mathematics and become a highly regarded math teacher.

As the players on the field pitched and batted balls, Steve shared a torrent of stories—one classroom experience after another where kids without hope were inspired and encouraged to become effective teachers and professionals in other math-related careers. Inning after inning I was surprised to find myself fighting back tears. I was deeply affected by Steve's passion and the influence it was having on so many young people.

"It is so important," said Steve, pounding his thigh. "Not just for students but for all of us. We all need to seek out and discover our inner greatness and to utilize our God-given talents. It's a philosophy the Math Corps teaches. That's why we emphasize mutual respect and the discovery of each individual's personal greatness. Yes, the Math Corps likely teaches math better than any other program in the country, but its real strength is in giving students self-confidence, self-esteem, mutual respect, and, most importantly, a desire to find the 'greatness within.'"

I was speechless. My emotions were overtaking me, my heart was pounding, and the roar in my head was so loud it drowned out the game, the crowd, and the stadium announcer. What an impact this man had had on others. Between innings and during every single pause in the conversation, I privately thanked God for Steve and for His message to me: "Find your greatness. Use it for the greatest good."

As I'd struggled with my future plans, I'd been troubled by the workaholic I had become even in retirement; I was neglectful of my family and of my spiritual development. But that day, I left the game changed. I simply had to discover my own "greatness." And in that greatness, I would no longer neglect my family or my spiritual development. Whatever this greatness was, I was absolutely certain of one thing—it was about touching the lives of others.

·············· *For Reflection* ··············

You are the light of the world. A town built on a hill cannot be hidden. Neither do people light a lamp and put it under a bowl. Instead they put it on its stand, and it gives light to everyone in the house. In the same way, let your light shine before others, that they may see your good deeds and glorify your Father in heaven.

Matthew 5:14–16

···

I'm certain God gave me the gift of this life-changing experience with Steve to encourage me to search for and discover my own personal greatness in a way I never seemed to have had time to pursue before. I hope sharing this story will motivate you to do the same, for your own greatness can become your gift to a world desperate for what you have to offer.

Each of us possesses spiritual gifts or "greatness" that we need to discern and then utilize. Have you seriously considered what your gifts are or what your "greatness" is? What are the gifts you possess and can offer to the world that have not yet been fully developed or exercised? What specific things will you do in the weeks or months ahead to impact other lives with your talents?

Jesus Himself beseeched his disciples in Matthew 5:14–16 to let their light shine forth instead of hiding it under a lamp bowl. You too can follow that time-proven advice. Discover your spiritual gifts and let them shine before others.

My Not-So-Secret Love

I first met Margaret Bradshaw after she had made a substantial gift to The American College in Bryn Mawr, Pennsylvania, where I served as chairman of the board of trustees. Since she lived in an apartment on Park Avenue just a few blocks from New York Life's offices where I worked, the college development officer encouraged me to visit and personally express the college's gratitude for her generosity.

It was an extremely hot summer day in August 2006, and I'd suffered a particularly sleepless night followed by a morning filled with difficult business meetings. Frankly, I was not in the mood to make the visit. But I had committed to it in advance, so I gathered myself together and rang the bell.

"Please follow me," said her housekeeper, escorting me to the living room—where I first witnessed Margaret, a diminutive lady surrounded by books, photographs, and various newspapers, comfortably seated and reading the *Wall Street Journal*. She looked up at me with a broad smile and raised her right arm to gently reach out and shake my hand. "What a pleasure to meet you, Mr. Sievert," she said. The heat of the apartment was only exceeded by the warmth of this engaging lady.

Even though she was a pioneer in our industry as the first female insurance agent for Boston's John Hancock Mutual Life Insurance Company, I knew Margaret was retired and didn't expect her to know much about recent events at New York Life. Was I ever wrong! Not only had she done her research on New York Life, but she'd learned all about me as well.

"Mr. Sievert," she respectfully addressed me as she discussed details about the company's sales growth, mentioned several key financial statistics, and congratulated me on both our well-conceived strategies and on my personal career success.

From there, she went on to deliberate recent developments in the insurance industry as well as local, state, and national politics, embarrassing me several times by asking my views on thought-provoking issues about which I knew nothing.

But the most interesting discussion revolved around Margaret's personal story—her historic involvement in the insurance industry and her extensive knowledge of American history. Margaret was only the fourth woman to become a licensed insurance agent in the United States, signing her first agent contract at the age of twenty-one. She recounted stories about her long career with John Hancock, including her efforts to break the gender barrier. All of this was incredibly interesting, but God had yet to reveal the most amazing thing about Margaret.

Just two months before our meeting, Margaret Bradshaw had celebrated her 101st birthday! This articulate centenarian had near-perfect recall of insurance industry milestones as well as historical events long before I was born. She read daily newspapers without the aid of eyeglasses, and her informed opinions were shaped and influenced by firsthand experiences.

In vivid detail, she described the thick manual she was given to study after signing her first agent's contract in 1926—eighty years earlier! To her great annoyance, the first page of the manual consisted of the company's written charge that all agents shave every morning. She smiled brightly, recalling how she'd shared her misgivings with the president of John Hancock—who quickly ordered numerous gender-based changes to the manual.

I laughed. "Margaret, that language shouldn't have surprised you. After all, it was only a few years after women's suffrage."

"You know, Mr. Sievert," she responded, "I never really got into that movement. Those broads were too radical for me!" (I later learned that although Margaret was a political conservative, she did indeed support women's suffrage and other women's rights issues.)

She then told me about a dinner meeting of the local agents' association in Providence, Rhode Island, in the early 1930s. As the first female president of the association, she was also one of the very few female members. Unfortunately, whoever planned the dinner chose an exclusive men's club for the venue. Not one to give up easily, Margaret essentially forced her way in by gaining support from many of the important male business leaders scheduled to attend the dinner. As a result, she was likely the first woman ever to be served a meal in that club and most certainly the first ever to preside over a business meeting there.

I glanced at my watch. I had a full schedule of meetings back at the office and had intended to spend no more than five to ten minutes with Margaret. But I was entranced; time stood still; and before I left—more than an hour later—Margaret insisted on giving me a framed picture of herself when she was in her late twenties.

What a beautiful young lady, I thought. But even looking on her flawless youth, I couldn't help but think how much more beautiful she was today. Her beauty shone clearly in her zeal for life, her recollection of historical events, her joy in the retelling of her story, and in what she continued to accomplish through her philanthropic passions.

A couple of months later, I had my second visit with this remarkable woman. This one revolved around events in American history. Margaret's recollections and perspective were enthralling. She spoke of her father, who owned a textile factory in Providence during World War I—and who refused to use the preferred German dyes because of Germany's involvement in the war. "My father was a 'real man,'" she told me. And a little later, to my delight and embarrassment, she said quite emphatically, "I like *real men*, Mr. Sievert, and I can tell—you're a *real man*."

"Please call me Fred," I implored her. "I insist." And there began—over the course of many more visits and phone calls—our unique and wonderful love affair.

On every call and visit, Margaret told me how much she loved me, and I returned the sentiment. She was very supportive of my decision to retire and go to divinity school, and she always asked about school and what I was learning. She took an interest in my wife's culinary education. And, of course, she loved to discuss current events.

Margaret was a philanthropist who generously supported many worthy causes. Through her church, she funded the building of schools in India and an array of projects, both domestic and abroad.

Inspired, I followed her lead. New York Life supported similar causes in Asia, and Sue and the kids and I had been discussing how to get more involved.

Through Margaret Bradshaw, God was infusing me with a new appreciation for life—as well as a vibrant example of what one can accomplish well after my comparatively young age of fifty-nine.

Two years after that initial meeting with Margaret, Sue and I were in Ireland for two weeks when a message arrived at our hotel:

Fred,

Would you mind doing me a favor and picking up a gift in Avoca's Shop at 13 Suffolk Street in Dublin? They're expecting you. Thank you, dearest.

Love, Margaret

I couldn't even remember telling her about the trip, but at 102 she had remembered and tracked us down.

On June 12, 2010, Sue and I spoke to Margaret on her 105th birthday. She expressed her love to both of us in her typical lucid and articulate fashion. During that call, she also ranted for some time about freewheeling government spending and the long-term consequences of the burgeoning national debt and annual deficits. Margaret was always thinking about the future and the longer-term implications of public policy.

I cherished every moment I spent with Margaret. I often thanked God for showing me how someone Margaret's age could touch the lives of so many. But I dreaded the inevitable.

I received the unwelcome phone call on a trip to Africa in 2011. Margaret died August 12 of that year at the age of 106. Thank God I had spoken to her just before we left. Thank God I'd enjoyed one last opportunity to tell her I loved her . . . to which she responded as she had so many times: "I just love you and Sue so much."

Margaret's life was indeed a unique journey and a life to celebrate. And even though I knew about many of her philanthropic benevolences,

I found out about one of her additional practices in a eulogy given at her funeral: Margaret read the newspaper daily and searched for people in the community who needed assistance. She then made anonymous gifts to ease their burdens. Not revealing this practice to anyone else, she concealed her love of the many others she helped. But I cannot hide my love the way she did; Margaret Bradshaw was my not-so-secret love.

.... *For Reflection* ....
He will call on me, and I will answer him; I will be with him in trouble, I will deliver him and honor him. With long life I will satisfy him and show him my salvation.

Psalm 91:15–16

As I began to plan for early retirement so I could pursue my passions, I needed to be reminded that life's journey does not end at age fifty-nine. I also needed to know I could positively impact thousands of lives through thoughtful activities after retirement—perhaps even more than I had before. I never really believed such an impact was possible until God introduced me to Margaret Bradshaw.

Our society unfortunately diminishes and often denigrates the wisdom and worth of the elderly. God often reveals wisdom to us through such individuals. Can you think of role models among the elderly during your lifetime? Are there any who stand out as people who shared their testimony and inspired you to improve yourself and to remain productive well beyond your working years? If there is no one living who fits that description, won't you identify ways in which you can reach out to an elderly person to tap into his or her wealth of knowledge and experience? How, when, and with whom will you do that? It could be as life-altering an experience for you as it was for me.

Margaret was able to impact countless lives through her support of her church and her philanthropy. As the Psalmist indicated in Psalm 91, even as a centenarian, God answered Margaret's call, delivered her,

honored her with long life, and showed her salvation. He will do the
same for you.

Erin's Story

It was 2002 and I was preparing for a visit to Vietnam in pursuit of a license for New York Life to do business in the country. As was customary, one of our local government relations employees made the arrangements for my various meetings and then accompanied me throughout my stay in the country. On this trip, my New York Life contact and guide was a lovely young Vietnamese lady named Erin Pham.

Like so many Americans of my generation, just the mention of "Vietnam" conjured up painful memories of a difficult period in history often magnified by the loss of a loved one. It was my first visit to the country, and as I prepared, I couldn't help thinking about one of my own best high school friends, Arnie Sarna, who died in combat. Arnie lived in my neighborhood, and during our junior and senior high school years we were inseparable. There were several other boys in the neighborhood with whom I hung around almost daily playing baseball, basketball, or football, but I had a special connection with Arnie. In addition to our regular talk about sports and girls, Arnie frequently engaged me in discussions about current events, politics, and even spiritual matters. We often pondered the meaning of life, the existence of God, and the mysteries of the universe and of creation. My fondest memories of Arnie were not the daytime athletic games but the evening walks around the neighborhood when we would ponder and debate more meaningful topics.

Arnie's passing was my first experience with the death of someone so close to me. I vividly remember my prolonged pain and grieving and the empathy I felt for his family when I attended his funeral. Just weeks before his death, he sent me a long, handwritten letter expressing his gratitude for our friendship and recalling many of the more memorable experiences we'd shared. He wrote that he couldn't wait to visit with me. I've kept that letter and still read it from time to time. Arnie did return to us—in a black body bag sent from Vietnam.

Even now, decades after the war ended, the very mention of "Vietnam" conjures up painful memories and thoughts for anyone who lived through that period: The daily body counts on both sides that were reported every evening on the network television news; the funeral processions; and the pain of losing a friend or family member for a cause that probably had more protestors than proponents in the United States. The war was very divisive on the home front, and that divisiveness made it particularly difficult for servicemen and women to return to a normal and productive life in the United States after completing their assignment in Vietnam.

And now, almost thirty years after the war had officially ended, I found myself wondering: What would Arnie look like had he survived? What career would he have pursued? Would we have remained friends and shared the wonderful experiences of raising families and having grandchildren? What would he think of me going to conduct business in Vietnam?

I was pleasantly surprised by the beauty of the Vietnamese landscape and the friendliness of the people. Evidently the scars of war and the devastating human losses suffered on both sides had largely healed but most certainly still resided in the hearts and minds of those most personally and directly affected, like those Vietnamese (North or South) who lost family members among the thousands of military or civilian casualties so coldly reported on the evening news every day.

Throughout my first day in Vietnam, Erin was by my side, briefing me on the key governmental and regulatory officials we would meet in each of several scheduled sessions. In all the rushing about to make our appointments, there was no time to discuss the history of the country, the war, or even her personal recollections of the aftermath. However, one evening, after a long day of meetings, we had an hour or so to chat during the ride to the airport. Though I had met with Vietnam's Minister of Finance and Deputy Prime Minister earlier in impressive ceremonial surroundings, the most memorable and inspiring discussion of the day took place during that drive.

After talking briefly about my own family and the adoption of my three daughters, I asked Erin about her background. What she told me moved me so much, that all these years later I asked her to share it with you through this book. Here is her response:

Dear Fred:

I have started to work on my story, and I feel great to write it. Funny how it all comes out so easily once I put my mind to it—as if the story has been waiting to be told. Thank you so much for giving me this opportunity to get in touch with a part of myself that I've kept bottled up for so long.

Kind Regards,

Erin

With her permission I have reprinted it here without embellishment. I am convinced God brought us together again so that Erin might inspire thousands of others with her miraculous story.

Glory to the Lord Who Saved Us from the Sea
by Erin Pham Steinhauer

My name is Erin Pham. I am forty years old this year. I am a wife, a mother of three, and have been a corporate businesswoman for twenty years. I was born in Saigon, Vietnam, at the height of the U.S.-Vietnam war, and left Vietnam on a wooden boat four years after the war ended. I have eleven brothers and sisters all living in the U.S. and countless nieces and nephews. My mother raised all of us on her own in America from the time we reached Lancaster, Pennsylvania, in 1979. My father was jailed by the Communist government at the end of the war and never reunited with his family.

This is a story about how God saved me and my family from going down into the Pacific Ocean in 1979. We escaped Vietnam to find freedom and reunite with our family in America. I was nine years old when we began our journey. At the time of our escape, over seventy percent of Vietnamese boats leaving Vietnam never reached their intended destinations; many were pillaged by Thai pirates (who did some of the worst things imaginable to refugee boat passengers) and the rest went down into the deep sea. Given the slim chance of survival, my mother's strategy was to divide the family into different groups that would leave at different times. My eldest brother and sister were the first to leave at ages sixteen and fourteen. Then, my fifteen-year-old older brother took my three-year-old younger brother with him. Then two other brothers and a sister went under the care of my aunt and uncle. Finally, my mother took the rest of her children. All in all, four different groups of boat people from 1975 to 1979. Given the risks of the journey and our being separated from the start, it was miraculous that we all survived and reunited in Lancaster, PA. Prior to the war, my family was considered one of the wealthiest in Saigon, and I lived in complete bliss without a day of worries. When we arrived in America, my mother had $2.50 in her pocket and a pack of twelve children from ages two to twenty-one.

For security reasons, we had kept the date and time of our escape secret until the last minute. And so, the night that we left Saigon, I was asleep in my bed when my aunt awakened me and told me to get dressed for the journey. I was very excited about the journey to America and, as a skinny little tomboy, I was ready for the promised great adventures that lay ahead. I put on my favorite jean shorts, a white polo shirt, and blue leather sandals. My siblings joined me; there were three sisters and my youngest brother (two years old) setting out that night on rickshaws. The drivers were waiting for us outside our grandmother's home as we were hiding out there. The night was unusually breezy and, as we rode through the nearly empty streets of Saigon, I looked closely at all the familiar sights. I wanted to take them in as much as I could because I knew that it was going to be the last time I'd ever see this beautiful city. At the same time, I felt an incredible sense of elation, excitement, and privilege to be so lucky to go to America. Certainly I did not know about the perilous road ahead before we would reach our final destination.

The rickshaws took us to an old stilt house built on a branch of the Saigon canal that leads to the river and eventually to the open sea. The eldest of my siblings traveling with us at the time was fifteen years old, and she directed us to go quietly onto a small covered wooden rowboat in the back of the house. We got in and hunched down, five little lumps with our heads down under the thick canvas roof that shielded us from outside view. A man and his wife began rowing the boat, pretending to be on a fishing trip, down the river towards our meeting point with my mother—she had to leave separately because we were considered "flight risks" and were under constant surveillance by the secret police.

About thirty minutes into the journey, a police patrol boat came alongside of us and began to ask questions about our destination. If we had been discovered, it would have been a disaster, as the punishment for escaping Vietnam was severe—imprisonment, torture, even death. Although we knew they wouldn't do this to kids, if we were caught, our mother would be in big trouble and we would not be able to continue our journey. The man rowing the boat joked to the police. "I am taking people to America!" he said and laughed, and somehow was able to convince them that he and his wife were just going to stake out some fishing locations. We were paralyzed by fear as we silently held our breath until the police were gone and out of sight.

We continued down the river and finally arrived at our destination at early dawn. We walked along a barren beach and came upon a wooded area where we saw our mother waiting at the edge with a big smile and open arms. We had made it to the "meeting point": Phase One of our journey was complete.

My mother explained that we would wait until dusk to go out on the "big boat that will sail us to America." I was anxious and shifty the rest of the day, and couldn't settle down no matter what I did, as I was filled with excitement thinking about this huge boat. I finally found some other kids to run around with and explore the dry, barren landscape.

Getting from the shore to the small rowboats that would take us to the larger transport boat was difficult. It was a fine evening, a bit windy, and the tides had receded about 100 yards out into the ocean, leaving a field of warm, squishy muddy swamp. At this point, I began to realize this wasn't going to be a joy ride to America. We all took our shoes off and trudged into the mud. My mother told us to hold on tightly to each other's arms in case someone could not pull himself or herself up from the thick mud. As we went, I felt the mud seep between my toes and rise up above my legs, knees, hands, arms, and chest. Suddenly, I heard my mother, who was carrying my two-year-old brother, let out a loud, terrified scream. She had seen a snake crawling on the surface nearby and panicked. She just stood frozen while my brother's screams joined hers. Fortunately, a friend came by to take my brother from her arms, extract me from the mud, and help all of us continue walking to the boat. Finally we reached water and waded in it for a while to clean the mud from our bodies, and then climbed into the small rowboats waiting to take us to the "big boat that would sail us to America."

While we sat in these small shuttle boats, the wind picked up and I suddenly felt a cold chill and started shaking. My sister Thu put her arms around me and we hugged to keep each other warm. It was dark by the time we came upon the "big boat that would sail us to America," and I was surprised to see so many little rowboats waiting to board the bigger boat. My mother started to freak out, saying, "There are too many people." The owner had promised that there would be less than half the number of people we now saw in the water, and he had taken substantial amounts of money for each passenger. But there was nothing else we could do at this point—either get aboard or go back.

The "big boat that would sail us to America" turned out to be a simple wooden boat with one main deck and an upper deck. We found a corner and sat down on the floor: my mother, four daughters, one son, two of a family friend's children, and my aunt—all wet and huddled together. As more and more people boarded the boat, we were pushed closer and closer to each other until all 200 or more passengers boarded a boat that was about six by seventeen meters. There were so many people that we only had enough floor space to sit back-to-back right next to each other, without being able to lie down. All our belongings were thrown off the boat, including all our valuables and any food that was not for the boat's crew. Even without baggage and food stores, there was no space to lie down or even to rest our backs to sleep. Yes, we had made it onto the "big boat that would sail us to America." Phase Two was completed but left us terrified.

And so we set off into the night, eager to leave our homes and to reach a destination unknown to us all. The first night was calm, but tense, as we navigated Vietnamese waters to reach international waters beyond the reach of Vietnamese authorities. The following morning, we were awakened by triple bad news: (1) the compass was missing, (2) we would be out of fuel in three days or less, and (3) we had thrown away most of the food so what we had—just rice—was only enough for about two days. Our chances of survival had just become even slimmer. Gloom settled over the boat, and yet a stubborn hope remained; we all knew there was no turning back at this point.

The hot sun beat down on us as we forged forward. I explored my surroundings and began to get to know people on the boat. Despite our mutual unspoken fears, everyone was nice, all with the same gleaming, sustaining hope in their eyes. My favorite place was the upper deck, where there was a little more room to maneuver and an ironically symbolic but reassuring big white cross. The presence of a symbol of God's love was reassuring but its display under these difficult and unchristian circumstances was very ironic. My mother didn't let me stay on the upper deck very long as it was not safe, and one could easily get thrown overboard into the water. That afternoon, there was an uproar. A child had fallen into the ocean as he was trying to go to the bathroom, which was off the back of the boat behind a wooden door. There were terrible cries from the child's mother, who grieved against a silent backdrop as everyone just sat and huddled together. As a result of this incident, the silent fears of the other children palpably filled the air.

When evening came, we began to hear the boat creak. There was talk of a leak in the wood hull, and people began to speculate that water would begin to come into the boat. Fear began to spread, and we hugged each other even closer. I slept very little that night, partly out of fear, but mostly because I was so uncomfortable from not being able to lie down. I nodded off a few times and dreamt of my comfortable bed at home.

On our second morning, I went to the upper deck and found that it was a cloudy grey day. The boat was rocking wildly, and I was amazed to see walls of rippled steel-grey waves that were at least as high as ten-story buildings. One after another, the waves kept rolling all around and underneath our little boat, which appeared ever tinier as the waves lifted and pulled us up and down like a yo-yo. At any moment, our boat could have been folded into these enormous waves, and we would have disappeared without a trace. Frightened, I came back down to my mother and just buried my face into her protective chest and cried.

Our boat moved wherever the great waves took us. On the open sea without a compass, we had no idea where we were or where we were headed. Nighttime came, and an eerie quiet blanketed the entire boat. The people just sat in silence, eyes open, perhaps waiting for fate to decide our future.

As predicted, on day three we ran out of food, and the boat had slowed and was sputtering, about to run out of fuel. The hope I had seen everywhere at the start of our journey was running out too, as all we could see around us was the endless sea, straight on to the horizon and beyond. My mother, the source of all our comfort and safety, looked desperate and helpless. She began to pray and cried silently to herself.

The day dragged on and on. People who were friendly earlier became edgy and irritable as hunger sunk in. I too was running out of energy and didn't feel like going around anymore; I just stayed with my mother or went to the upper deck to look at the waves. It seemed America was an awfully long way away, too far for any of us to reach from this tiny boat. I started daydreaming of the reunion with my brothers and sisters waiting for us in America, of eating delicious food, of swimming in the ocean alongside the boat, of angels flying above. In the evening, we began to feel violent rocking, signs of a storm coming our way. The storm lasted all night and into the morning.

When day broke on the fourth morning, the rain was still falling, and the sea continued its relentless rocking. This day we saw a big orange ship in the distance—hope for rescue. Women and children went to the upper deck. I waved my arms as fast as I could and called out for the people on the ship to come and help us. The ship stood in the same place for hours, and by noon, it had started to move away from us.

In that moment, all hope was lost. Chaos spread throughout the boat as people knew we were close to reaching the end. It seemed like all 200 people were making noise at the same time, either praying out loud to their gods, crying to one another, or saying their good-byes. My mother was also praying, saying she regretted that she had brought her children to their deaths. Some time passed, and as the noise calmed down, a boy traveling with us pointed to the wall of the boat and cried out, "Look! I think the god of the sea is coming to rescue us!" We all said he was hallucinating and paid no attention. Just as he repeated the same thing again, someone on the upper deck said, "The big orange ship is coming for us!"

I ran up as fast as I could and saw the ship moving quickly in our direction, and heard cries of happiness all around me. Many people gathered around the big white cross on our boat, thanking the Lord Jesus Christ for saving us. I was so glad the big orange boat changed its mind and came to rescue us! When the ship came upon us, it looked like a giant city made of steel compared to our tiny wooden boat. Rope ladders dropped down and huge white men descended from the ship. They grabbed us children two at a time and climbed back up to put us on the massive steel deck. Up and down they went carrying people up to the boat. I was amazed at how big and strong they were, just like in the Western movies. There were other nice people on the ship handing out water and food to everyone.

The next few hours were the most amazing part of the journey. The storm picked up and rain came down hard. I stood on the deck of the ship looking down at our now tiny empty wooden boat getting tossed around from side to side, and after a while, the boat sank below the sea. I couldn't believe it. We were saved by the grace of God and by the people on this big orange ship who turned around to rescue us when they knew we were not going to make it through the storm. We all stood frozen in silence, thankful to be alive. My mother said she felt as though she had died and come back to life again.

We must have smelled bad because we were all lined up and escorted into the bathrooms for long soapy showers. We were given food and places to sleep. The next few days were a blur. I walked around exploring the ship and learned that it was called "Brimminger," an oil tanker from

Norway. I made friends with the nice people onboard and was even given fifteen dollars by a nice man who said to keep it for when we would need to use it in America.

After three days on Brimminger, we anchored in Singapore, and were processed at the immigration camp where we stayed for three months while we waited for sponsorship papers from Lancaster, PA. We were fortunate to have been sponsored by a family who were members of a church in Lancaster. They had learned about us through Catholic Relief Services and decided they wanted to help reunite our family.

We finally arrived in America in December 1979. It was evening when the airplane landed in Lancaster. I looked outside the window and saw a frozen land blanketed with white snow. I was filled with anticipation to see my siblings' home in America. When we walked out into the terminal, we saw our family and members of the church waving and smiling at us. It was an amazing sight after all that we went through to get there. My mother broke down and sobbed as she hugged and kissed each of her children. I was so happy to see my family that I ran to hug and kiss them. It felt as if we were whole again, and that we could now restart our lives in a land of endless possibilities. After a while, we noticed that we had forgotten the church people, and shook their hands and introduced ourselves to them. My mother thanked them for helping us, and we all went to my aunt's home. We stayed there for a few weeks while looking for a home to rent that would accommodate all of us; it was difficult, but we found a four-bedroom row house on News Street.

Our first few years in America were not as easy as we had expected. In addition to restarting life in a completely new land, which is hard enough, my mother had to figure out how to do this with twelve young children. Moreover, my mother had very few domestic skills, since she was a career businesswoman, and in Vietnam had had maids and nannies to help her with family matters.

While we had help from the church, my mother later told me she felt completely hopeless and desperate as she wondered how we would make it in America with the little means that we had (my older siblings worked, but initially we had to receive welfare assistance from the government). Then she received a call from a minister from the Vietnamese church who said he had heard about our family and wanted to help. My mother jumped for joy to speak with someone in Vietnamese and invited him to our home. The minister told her that he couldn't sleep, thinking about our family's trouble, and said he felt a spiritual need (perhaps even a message from God) to come and talk to us. He told us God loved us and would keep us safe if we relied on him. My mother immediately accepted Jesus Christ as her savior and from that point on we all began to regularly attend church and worship our God.

Since then, while we still experienced hardship during the first few years in America, we always made it through all the situations and difficulties that challenged us. Most of us ended up with college degrees and now have careers and children of our own.

Years later, I was the first family member who went back to Vietnam, just weeks after I graduated from George Washington University. Flying over the ocean to reach Vietnam's coastline was one of the most emotional moments of my life. All the memories of the boat and being rescued on the big orange ship came back like it had happened only yesterday. Tears just poured down my face and I couldn't help but to pray to God, giving thanks for what God had done for me on that day fifteen years before.

My first opportunity to move back to Vietnam was in 2004, when I took a position as chief representative with The New York Life Insurance Company (where I still work). Another wonderful gift from God was that as if by a miracle, my New York Life office was located directly across the street from where my mother had operated her business in Central Saigon, and where I had spent many days as a child playing on the streets. It was like God wanted to remind me that I had been given a second chance—to begin where my mother left off, to restart a career and a new life for myself, and for her.

I give thanks to God every day for my family's survival and for allowing me to live this miracle.

And I, Fred Sievert, thank God that this lovely woman worked for me at New York Life. I thank God too that in the midst of a busy schedule, in a car ride to the airport, she revealed her miraculous story to me so that I might bring some degree of closure to my grief over a long-lost friend. In a strange but wonderful way, the survival of Erin and her family rendered Arnie's short life more meaningful. Perhaps the loss of so many Americans and Vietnamese provided a gateway for many thousands of refugees to be liberated from the oppressive regime of the North and also brought many to a faith in Jesus Christ as a result of God's blessings in the liberation process.

·············· *For Reflection* ···············

So do not fear, for I am with you; do not be dismayed, for I am your God. I will strengthen you and help you; I will uphold you with my righteous right hand.

Isaiah 41:10

··

I was indeed blessed in a business setting to learn of the miraculous story of Erin Pham. I am certain God wanted me to hear Erin's story—both to heal my grief over a friend I thought had been lost in vain and also to renew my faith in a living God who performs miracles around the globe for all people.

You may not have a story quite as fantastic as Erin's, but my guess is you have had experiences in which God facilitated a transition in your life that had a positive long-term impact. Just as your life is enriched and your faith is reinforced by hearing the stories others tell of experiences in which they felt close to God, others can be impacted by your stories. In fact, writing this book has been my way of relating my own encounters with God in an effort to touch the lives of my readers.

Erin's story is a great example of how, as stated in Isaiah 41, we should not fear and we can trust in God to strengthen and uphold us in His righteous hand. Erin believes, as I do, that God miraculously reunited her large family intact after facing enormous life-threatening risks while escaping Vietnam and traveling the high seas in refugee boats.

Recall those incidents in your life in which you experienced fear but came through it in miraculous fashion. Consider the possibility that God had an important role in making that happen. Have you shared your own story with others? Commit now to retelling stories that fortified your faith so your stories might inspire others.

Chapter 2 Exercises

Chapter 2 told stories of experiences in which God spoke to me or revealed truths through existing friends and new acquaintances. This has happened many times throughout my life and, as a result, I am now always tuned in to what God might be telling me through people I fortuitously meet or through reunions with those I haven't seen in many years. I also recognize that I can be the friend through whom God speaks to others.

Divine Messages Delivered through Friends

My reunion with my friend Warren after a thirty-year separation changed the future course of my life and resulted in a very fulfilling early retirement. It is no exaggeration to say that this book would not have been written but for that reunion.

- Can you identify just one person from your past with whom you enjoyed a strong friendship and in whose presence you felt spiritually enriched?
- Describe how they made you feel and why it was a spiritual experience.
- If you could locate them, what would you say to them?
- Using today's Internet search capabilities, try to find them and have that conversation if you can. God may just have very pleasant surprises in store for both of you.

A Life Lived Well

My centenarian friend Margaret Bradshaw showed me that life doesn't end at age fifty-nine or upon retirement from active employment. Margaret was positively impacting lives until the day she died at age 106. Her faith and her philanthropy were an inspiration to me and to many others as we sought our own post-retirement passions.

- Whether or not you have ever gone through a formal discernment exercise, try now to identify and list your greatest passions and your God-given spiritual gifts.
- Honestly assess the extent to which you are utilizing those gifts and following those passions.
- Dream a little about your future and identify the ways in which you will proactively pursue your passions and use those gifts to advance God's Kingdom in the future. It's a journey that can only lead to happiness and fulfillment.

Tailor-Made Testimonies

My work-related visit to Vietnam with Erin Pham as my guide resulted in my hearing her remarkable story of God's grace in her family's escape from Vietnam following the war. Prior to contributing to this book, she had never recorded the story in writing to share her almost tailor-made testimony in a way that would positively impact many other lives.

- Think back on a time when you palpably felt the presence of God in your life. It need not be a dramatic conversion experience; rather, it might just be an experience in which you knew that God was uplifting you and pouring out His love.
- Describe the experience by jotting down some notes about the circumstances of the encounter, how you felt, and why.
- Share this experience with your study group, your spouse, or a friend. You may even be more comfortable sharing it with a recent acquaintance (as Erin did with me). If you do this, I believe you will feel very gratified knowing that God may be speaking to your friends and acquaintances through you.

Chapter 3

GOD REVEALED . . .

AT THE CROSSROADS
IN OUR LIVES

· ·

W e have all had experiences when a single decision or event was pivotal to the future path we'd follow in our life's journey. At many of those important crossroads, we seemingly had total control over our own actions or decisions and could thereby determine our own destiny—for better or worse.

At other times, we may have had little or no control—those experiences include things like being involved in accidents, suffering the loss of a loved one, being unfairly accused of a wrongdoing, falling victim to a violent crime, sustaining physical or mental abuse, or enduring unforeseen challenges in our personal or business lives. Depending on the ultimate outcome, we may have felt the experience occurred purely by chance. In other cases, we may have believed that God had a hand in orchestrating something that seemed too coincidental to have occurred by chance. And in some, we may have felt God abandoned us in our time of greatest need.

In this chapter, I relate four stories that represent pivotal moments in my life. The impact on my emotional well-being, my career, or my personal life had the potential to be either devastatingly negative or extraordinarily positive.

As you read these stories, think of episodes in your life where you came to crossroads—times when the future trajectory of your life path was reset. Do you think that realignment involved God's guidance or was it entirely of your own doing? And in the future, will you be more attuned to similarly critical moments?

Tragedy Interrupted

I was thirteen years old and living a happy life with two hard-working parents and my nine-year-old brother, Rob. We were a one-car family and in 1961 we owned a relatively new 1957 Ford Fairlane.

Our house was a modest three-bedroom ranch-style home in a self-contained Midwestern neighborhood where houses were close—separated only by driveways leading to detached two-car garages—and we knew our neighbors well.

In this post-war baby boom era, our community of twenty-five or thirty similar homes was always bustling with children of all ages. Most families had three or four and some even more. No one locked their doors at night; it was comfortable and safe; and there was very little through traffic, so we often played in the streets.

Almost every day of the year, regardless of the season or weather, we boys could be found playing baseball, football, or basketball. I had no sisters, so I don't recall what the girls were doing, but they played too. It was the children who tied the families together; our play represented the social nexus and vibrancy of the community.

Next door to us was the Steggles family. Their children were mostly younger than me and my brother, and we knew all of them well—three boys and a girl, ranging in age from two to ten. We talked and bantered over the chain link fence that separated our yards. The two oldest Steggles boys were frequent participants in whatever sport we were playing, and the two-year-old received a great deal of attention and affection from everyone in the neighborhood.

One very hot and humid midsummer day, after a competitive nine-inning baseball game, I trotted home dripping with sweat and covered with dirt. It was too uncomfortable to continue our game, but I was sure we'd return to the field when the temperature dropped in the late afternoon. In Michigan, dusk occurred after 9 p.m., and games ended when it was simply too dark to see the ball.

At thirteen, I didn't even consider a midday shower so, wet and filthy, I relaxed on the couch in our small living room and watched a soap opera on the black-and-white television. There was no air conditioning but a small fan kept the air circulating and dried me as I began to doze off.

"Hey, Freddy," said my dad, jolting me out of slumber, "do you want to go to the store with me?"

"Yes!" I shouted, instantly reviving. I rarely got time alone with my dad, who worked extremely long hours, and this was an opportunity I could not pass up.

How different things would have been if he hadn't invited me or if I had opted for sleep and declined his offer.

Our car was parked in the driveway, and we approached from the front of the vehicle. Dad got in on the driver's side and I jumped into the passenger seat from the other side. Dad turned on the ignition.

I didn't hear a voice, I wasn't thinking about any possible problem, and I hadn't seen anything unusual as I got into the car. But just as Dad was putting the transmission into reverse, I yelled, "Stop!"

Startled by my outburst, he instinctively stomped on the brake pedal and forced the gearshift lever back into Park.

"I need to check something," I told him, jumping out of the car.

Not knowing what I'd find, I hurried behind the car and looked underneath. To my shock and amazement, there was the Steggles toddler from next door. He was sleeping. His position in the car's shadow had protected him from the hot sun—and his head was directly behind the rear tire on the driver's side.

Shaken by what had almost happened, Dad scooped up the baby and gently cradled him while walking next door to explain to the baby's mother. We were all so relieved that we didn't even ask how the child had gotten there.

I have no explanation for the warning I received other than God's intervention. I can scarcely comprehend what could have happened and how horrible it could have been for the Steggles family, for my dad, and for me. I am certain my own life would have evolved differently had I struggled with the guilt of such a disaster. There is no question in my mind that God chose to intervene in saving the life of this sweet child on that hot summer day in 1961.

············ *For Reflection* ··············

The Lord will keep you from all harm— he will watch over your life; the Lord will watch over your coming and going both now and forevermore.

Psalm 121:7–8

···

Horrible accidents that unexpectedly take beloved family members, friends, or lovers happen every day. I'm not sure we ever fully recover from such losses, particularly when they could have been avoided or prevented. I believe that God can—and often does—intervene in such situations, but I don't know why He doesn't do so more often. Why some live while others die—and some suffer while others flourish—are questions with which we all struggle. Perhaps the answer is that even in our grief we grow spiritually and emotionally and thereby come closer to our God. Nonetheless, we still cry out to God and ask "Why?" when the pain is so overwhelming.

I know from personal experience that it's through episodes of physical pain and emotional suffering that we grow and develop into more mature, well-balanced, and resilient beings capable of sharing experiences and serving others in need of emotional support.

In any event, we shouldn't allow our grief in some situations to overcome our joy in others. I trust in God's wisdom and believe our experiences, both joyful and dreadful, have a divine purpose. With that knowledge and faith, we should rejoice and praise God when He intervenes on our behalf in a glorious way as He did for me and my father in that potentially disastrous trip to the store in 1961.

Have you ever had an experience in which God's intervention seemed abundantly clear to you? Do you wonder how your life and the lives of others have been altered by that providential experience? Although you may not have understood it at the time, or even seen it as divinely influenced, can you now surmise why God intervened? And do you believe, as I do, that you can trust in Him to watch over you and keep you from harm, as suggested in Psalm 121?

A Math Teacher in the Girls' Locker Room

After graduating from college in 1970, following my passion to impact the lives of young people, I taught junior high school mathematics and photography in Wayne, Michigan. It was gratifying to teach not only an academic discipline but also an artistic one—especially since photography is one of my favorite avocations. After school I also coached football, wrestling, and track, which allowed me to see and interact with students in a different and fulfilling capacity.

Often I drove home with a smile, contemplating how I had done my part to help change the world from the bottom up by positively influencing even the very small subset of America's youth enrolled at Franklin Junior High School. But, much to my frustration, my efforts were often sabotaged by an undisciplined and dysfunctional environment.

You see, the principal of Franklin had an almost neurotic need to be loved by the students, so teachers sending students to his office often found themselves embroiled in an argument—with him defending even the most egregious behaviors. Since the students knew this, there was no deterrent to inappropriate behavior.

One afternoon during an after-school home basketball game, things came to a head. The visiting team was using the girls' locker room to change clothes and secure their belongings. While the game was being played, some Franklin students entered the locker room and stole their watches and money.

Understandably livid at the lack of security, the visiting coach reported the stolen valuables immediately following the game. I had attended the game, and the next morning when I learned of the theft, I recalled seeing a couple of our students who had particularly bad behavioral records hanging around that locker room during the game. Reporting this to the principal, I suggested we call the students to the office for questioning.

"Absolutely not," said the principal. "You have no definitive proof. I will not antagonize potentially innocent students based on suspicion alone."

Predictable. Nonetheless, I was extremely frustrated. After all, we were talking about a criminal offense, and he seemed unwilling to even investigate. This was the last straw. I was determined to do whatever I could to gather proof of student misbehavior to support tough disciplinary action moving forward. But what could I do?

After much contemplation, I got an idea. The best place to start my detective work would be at the next home basketball game. My plan was so ingenious it would make it impossible for the principal to avoid confrontation with suspected culprits. Before the next home game, I secretly prepared my thirty-five–millimeter camera with a paparazzi-style zoom lens and large flash attachment. When I arrived with it at the gym, I waited in the hallway outside the girls' locker room for the visiting team to dress and go out to the court. Many students and faculty members saw me but no one gave me a second glance—there was nothing suspicious about the photography teacher carrying camera equipment to a sporting event. But instead of entering the gym to stake out the best spot for game photographs, I waited. And as soon as all spectators had gone into the gym to watch the game and the hallway was empty, I surreptitiously entered the locker room totally unnoticed. I was in!

Carefully, quietly, I strategically positioned myself in the first of several open shower stalls that provided a perfect view of the long row of lockers. I could barely wait to see the fear on the faces of those Franklin students caught on camera in the act of pilfering the opposing team's temporary lockers. A rush of excitement came over me. How satisfying it would be to produce the incontrovertible proof the principal had demanded—proof that would finally force him to act responsibly. For several minutes, I quietly waited until I finally heard the locker room door open. This was it—I would shortly have proof! My heart pounded as I heard lockers opening and closing. One last check: yes, my camera settings were appropriate. And slowly I leaned out of the shower stall with my eye in the viewfinder, ready to focus and snap a series of pictures of the thieves in the act of greedily emptying the pockets and wallets of the visiting team's clothing.

To my horror, instead of delinquents, there were girls! About fifteen of them from the volleyball team, and they were changing out of their uniforms, standing there in their bras and panties. I'd had no warning—they'd been absolutely silent, probably because they had just lost their volleyball match.

My heart racing, I darted back into the stall as quietly as I could and began to think. There was nowhere to hide: there were no shower curtains on these stalls and I was in the one closest to the lockers. If even *one girl* decided to take a shower, I would be discovered. If I yelled out to reveal myself, surely the girls would recognize my voice. Even if they didn't, hearing a male voice in the locker room would cause mass hysteria. Some girls might rush out of the locker room unclothed, to even greater embarrassment, while others might scream or summon the coach. They would then wait outside the locker room for the pervert, only to see Mr. Sievert, the math and photography teacher, emerge with his powerful camera equipment. What if I instead remained silent and risked confrontation with one or more totally naked junior high school girls stepping into the shower stall and encountering their math teacher, crouched down on the tile floor, clutching his impressive camera outfit? But maybe it wouldn't happen. After all, girls that age might be too embarrassed by their pubescent bodies to take a shower in an open stall.

I would remain silent. I crouched in the corner, praying and waiting for what seemed to be an eternity, until finally I heard the sounds of zipping duffel bags and banging locker doors, gradually fading away to complete silence. My heartbeat slowed and the blood began to flow once again into my white knuckles. When I was certain no one remained in the locker room, I slipped out totally unnoticed.

Mortified that I'd done something so stupid, I didn't tell anyone—not even my wife—about the incident for two or three years. Later, sufficiently distanced from the ordeal, I did reveal it to my wife and a couple of my fellow teachers. At a teachers' reunion more than thirty years later, I learned that my story had become part of the school folklore, at least among the faculty.

How would my life and career have changed if just one girl had decided to take a shower? I suspect I would have been fired or suspended or much worse. Who would have ever believed my story of doing legitimate detective work in the girls' locker room? And how would the courts have viewed it if any of those girls' parents had pressed charges? And how could I blame them? Being the father of three girls myself, I probably would have had little sympathy or tolerance for such inexplicable behavior by a junior high school teacher.

In hindsight I realize that it was my selfish and obsessive need to overpower the principal's need to be loved that blinded me to the obvious reality that girls might enter the girls' locker room and foil my plan. How incredibly foolish.

It was evident God was protecting me. I have thanked Him countless times over the years for allowing me to escape that nightmarish situation and the devastating impact it most certainly would have had on my life.

·············· *For Reflection* ··············
When Jesus landed and saw a large crowd, he had compassion on them, because they were like sheep without a shepherd. So he began teaching them many things.

Mark 6:34

··

The locker room story is just one of many I could recount in which I believe God took a part in sparing me or other members of my family from tragic outcomes. At other times, tragedy *did* strike, as it does for all of us. When the worst happens, I pray to God for answers. When the answers aren't forthcoming, my faith sustains me in the belief that those answers will eventually come. I also find myself praying often to God to protect friends and family members before they encounter difficult or dangerous situations.

The passage from the Gospel of Mark speaks of Jesus compassionately teaching the crowd that was described as "sheep without a shepherd." Lost sheep often find themselves caught somewhere, faced with dangers they never anticipated, and unable to find a way out on their own. There probably is no better way to describe how I felt in that locker room shower stall.

Have you had dangerous encounters or episodes in your life that could have significantly jeopardized your future? Have you been faced with seemingly insurmountable problems for which you saw no solutions? Did you reach out to God in prayer as you faced those difficult situations? Do you believe that God will protect you, love you, and guide you as a shepherd when you are like a lost sheep unable to find your way?

A Career Turning Point

In 1981, following my early actuarial training in Boston at the John Hancock Mutual Insurance Company, I moved our young family back to the Detroit area to accept a position at a smaller firm, Maccabees Mutual Life Insurance Company. It was a vocationally challenging move but one with significant upside potential.

The challenge was that not only was this my first real managerial position, but some of the people I was managing were much older than I.

With single-minded focus, emulating my father's work ethic, I drove ahead—my eye always on the upside potential: promotions, more responsibilities, more lofty titles, and, yes, more compensation.

Did I succeed? Well, by my worldly criteria, yes. I was given more and more responsibilities almost annually and received several promotions in a short period. For eleven years (1981 through 1991), I sped down my "career path" at Maccabees. From a purely financial role in a single product line, I advanced to oversee the financial work for several business units and later added product design and development for multiple product lines.

Although I was neglecting my family and my spiritual development during this period of advancement, I could not turn off my tendency to reflect, so during this period I also learned a lot. As I watched people campaign for promotions or enhanced job responsibilities for all the wrong reasons, I realized I too did this. I was part of a generation that sought impressive titles and increased compensation at the expense of delaying the pursuit of passions, skills, and experiences that would ultimately provide happiness and fulfillment. In exchange for an impressive title or more money, we were willing to accept assignments for which we were unqualified—even knowing that we'd likely be challenged, frustrated, and unhappy. It was the culture. And as I watched others self-destruct along this path—and, as their manager, even had to dismiss them for it—it finally occurred to me that the same fate could befall me.

I resolved to change: I stopped aggressively pursuing promotions and greater responsibilities and, instead, I simply did my best in the job I held and relied on God to find the next logical career move for me in a way that would ultimately impact the most lives and do the most good for the company and its customers. This decision marked the beginning of a period of ongoing catharsis, and I found myself spending more time daily with my family and in prayer and Bible study. I still worked long hours but it seemed that my productivity increased and my desire to advance, though not completely sated, was diminished and of far less importance.

I was fortunate that at this critical juncture in my career I was reporting to the CEO and president, Jules Pallone. Jules was a soft-spoken leader who far more often provided positive rather than negative feedback and expressed encouragement rather than disappointment. Under his management style, I thrived.

My responsibilities were huge, but I attempted to do my best. I continued to hire good people and delegate effectively, allowing me to manage through successively increasing responsibilities without serious personal burden. I leveraged my skills by maintaining a team of superstar subordinates who I trusted to effectively manage their functions.

As my lifestyle improved, I remember talking to a friend in California: "I'm doing it, Al. Really. It's everything I intended. I'm climbing so fast, I can't believe it; I'm finally comfortable financially. And you know what? I'm really not interested in taking on more responsibility. I can't believe I'm saying this."

But it was my truth: I felt I had reached a better balance in my work, family, and spiritual life, and I was happier than I had been in some time.

But nothing stays the same for long. Shortly after I'd settled into this comfortable spot, Jules Pallone called me into his office. "Fred," he said, "I want you to take on something new. I want to add sales and marketing to your areas of responsibility. It's a major promotion."

I was scared. I wasn't even sure I wanted the lofty title and responsibilities that attached to this new role. But the thought of my recent successes coupled with this enormous challenge once again stirred my ambition.

But before I could answer, something unexpected happened. Suddenly this soft-spoken, normally gentle man turned stern, worried even. "There's something else, Fred. I've got to be straight with you. I'm taking a risk here because, to be quite blunt, I'm not sure you're up to the challenge."

I listened intently, aware that most likely he had no idea that I shared his reservations.

"I've had to think long and hard about offering you so much responsibility. I'm going to get backlash from many of the older executives who consider themselves candidates for this position. You know what they're going to say? 'Fred Sievert? He's an actuary and a financial executive. He has no experience in sales and marketing.' And that's not all."

I listened even harder, sensing that this was something important for me to hear.

"They aren't the only ones who aren't sure about this. I'm concerned about your ability to step up. You're going to have to work very hard to build the appropriate rapport and respect of the sales and marketing officers and employees. Otherwise," he said, "I'm afraid you will fail."

Jules was a very thoughtful, considerate, and compassionate man, and I knew these words were difficult for him to articulate. But they were necessary and they hit me hard.

Instantly I knew I could not turn down this promotion and my own fear of failure transformed into a great motivator. Why had Jules given me such a harsh truth? Somehow he knew that, *for me*, his truthfully voiced doubts were the exact challenge and motivation I needed to invest the time and energy required to succeed.

"I will do my best. Thank you, Jules," I replied. But as I left his office, I was hit by yet another worry: would I relapse into my former lifestyle in the process? And almost as quickly, I got the answer. For the past several years, I'd prayed and trusted God to direct my career path. He would see me through this change too.

I'm convinced that God knew I needed to be challenged and at the exact right time He used Jules Pallone as His messenger. Because I think it was God who had bigger things in store for me.

The promotion from Jules marked a turning point onto a path that I believe was foreordained by God. The progression of my responsibilities at Maccabees was followed by a remarkably similar career path at a much larger company. The experience gained in a mid-sized company like Maccabees was perfect training and on-the-job experience for moving into the big time—New York Life Insurance Company, a Fortune 100 company, where I worked from 1992 until my retirement in 2007.

And most important, this path enabled me to realize a far greater purpose: As my job expanded so did my platform. At both Maccabees and then later at New York Life, having management responsibility for a very large and dedicated field force of agents and sales managers enabled me to greatly increase my circle of influence and share my faith and my numerous encounters with God.

There certainly was much more work to be done to correct my work and family life imbalance. But, at this point in my career, I was grateful that God knew exactly what I needed both professionally and spiritually and delivered the transformative message so effectively through the voice of my boss, mentor, and friend, Jules Pallone.

·············· *For Reflection* ···············
I will lead the blind by ways they have not known, along unfamiliar paths I will guide them; I will turn the darkness into light before them and make the rough places smooth. These are the things I will do; I will not forsake them.

Isaiah 42:16

··

When people ask me to identify the turning point of my career, I don't hesitate. It was the big promotion at Maccabees and the words from Jules Pallone. He had enough confidence in me to promote me but at the same time warn me of the risk of failure. His candor in sharing his concerns that the role might be beyond my capabilities was just the incentive I needed to prove him wrong. What I didn't realize at the time, however, was that God was positioning me for future roles that would provide a platform for demonstrating and expressing my faith to a far broader audience.

Have there been critical crossroads in your life when you (or someone with an element of control over your destiny) had to make important decisions that would materially affect your future? Think back on decisions like your choice of a college, your job changes, your geographical moves, and even your choice of a spouse. In hindsight, did any of those decisions significantly impact your future? Does it seem to you now that God may have had a hand in positioning you for that future? Did any of those outcomes produce opportunities to share your faith or grow in your own spiritual development? If so, you can bet God had a hand in overcoming obstacles and in transitioning beyond those pivotal decisions. We can trust in the assurances of divine guidance provided in Isaiah: "He will make the rough places smooth."

Lessons for the Affluent in Africa

In 2004, my oldest son, Zac, graduated from high school and together we took a two-week trip to Botswana, South Africa, and Zimbabwe.

The son of a successful New York City executive, Zac grew up in the very affluent environment of Fairfield County, Connecticut. He and all his friends had the kinds of luxuries, exciting experiences, and material possessions about which most American teens can only dream. He was very popular in high school, and as a senior he captained both his football and lacrosse teams.

If you think that sounds like an idyllic situation, think again. Like so many other advantaged youth, Zac suffered for years from depression; he never seemed to be happy or to enjoy life. I had hoped and prayed that this trip might be therapeutic because it offered the chance for him to enjoy his two greatest passions: photography and herpetology.

I shared Zac's passion for photography; additionally, I was interested in observing African wildlife, so this trip was exciting for both of us. We took thousands of digital photos and, even though it was winter in South Africa, we encountered a number of snakes and other reptiles.

In Singita, a luxurious camp in Kruger National Park, South Africa, we enjoyed twice-a-day jeep safaris. On our first day we observed at close range all of the "big five" game animals—lions, leopards, African elephants, rhinos, and Cape buffalo. On the first night, we saw a mother cheetah feeding her two cubs and then watched as a pride of lions fed on a freshly killed wildebeest. Our proximity to the ferociously aggressive lions was daunting; we watched from an open jeep only ten or fifteen feet away, within clear sight, sound, and smell of the animals.

On the second day we asked the guides if we could search for snakes. Even though they told us it was highly unlikely that we would see any snakes in the winter, within a few minutes of leaving camp, Zac and our guide were on foot, tracking a fifteen-foot python. The guide held his rifle ready as Zac actually touched the python's tail as it slithered through tall grass and up a rocky ledge.

As thrilling as these experiences were, they were not the defining aspect of the trip for either of us. That came the afternoon we left our luxurious camp between scheduled jeep excursions and a guide took us and two other guests to a fairly primitive local village. Surrounded by fences, the village was protected from dangerous wild game; the homes ranged from cinder-block construction to grass huts with dirt floors. We had never seen anything like this community in the United States, and it seemed like something from a National Geographic television program.

Upon our arrival, we went to the villagers' makeshift preschool; about forty children ranging in age from three to five were attending. We were charmed by these personable, happy children as they sang and acted out nursery school songs for us. We were especially impressed that they sang to us in English. One of the songs was written to the tune of "Old McDonald Had a Farm," but their version was all about wild game animals. We were delighted as, after each chorus, a different youngster stepped forward to do a solo, imitating the sounds of wild game.

Next we watched, amazed, as the adult women of the village prepared meals with very primitive utensils. This was not a historical demonstration of how villagers used to prepare food; this was how the women currently prepared daily meals for the village—without any of the modern, sophisticated appliances found in the typically well-equipped kitchens of Fairfield County!

With great pride and joy, the senior men of the village then walked us into a small hut that served as a makeshift museum of local history and ancestry. These gentlemen could not speak English, but with obvious delight, they gave us many treasured artifacts to handle and admire. The museum housed everything from formal headdresses and nose rings to musical instruments and weapons of war. Because many of the artifacts were dusty and damaged, I couldn't help but think that the typical residents of my Connecticut neighborhood might have discarded these valued possessions as worthless pieces of rubbish.

To conclude our visit, we were seated outside in the hot midday sun and given a cold, refreshing drink. We were then treated to an adult male dancing group in traditional ceremonial dress followed by a young men's singing group in much more modern, colorful dress. None of their songs were in English, but somehow we could distinguish love songs from ballads from songs of celebration simply by the rhythm, tone, and expressions on the faces of the singers.

The one common denominator in every delightful experience of our visit to the village was the hospitality of every person we met. All were visibly pleased to have us visit—and all of them, no matter what age, demonstrated the same joy and friendliness of the preschool kids.

After leaving the sumptuousness of our camp at Singita, we headed to Mombo Camp in Botswana, where the game viewing was even more spectacular. There, we saw four to five times more wildlife and were filling our four-gigabyte digital cards on every jeep ride.

Part of the routine at Mombo Camp was for the guests from all nine cabins to dine together at one large candle-lit oval table, after which we sat around a campfire and shared stories of the day's experiences. On our last evening, we gathered around the table. The sun had set and the temperature had dropped to a cool but comfortable level; the dinner was interrupted often by the evening calls of various wild game animals. We often heard the roaring of lions, the snorting of hippos, and the trumpeting of elephants.

Although there were only about twenty guests, they were an interesting and diverse collection of characters from around the globe. In addition to the Mombo Camp hosts, our group was comprised of a family of five from New Jersey with three college-age children; two older couples, one from Australia and another from California; and two middle-aged sisters from Britain who were getting away together for the first time in decades. Dinner seating was intentionally mixed, with guests mingling around the table. I was seated across the table and a few seats away from Zac.

At a lull in the conversation, I heard one of the older adult guests ask Zac what the highlight of the trip had been for him. I expected Zac to talk about the wild game, the incredible photo opportunities, or his tracking of the big python.

"It was the visit to the village outside Singita," he answered.

"Really?" responded the older gentleman. "Why was it so special for you?"

"Because the people were so *happy*," said Zac simply. "They had absolutely nothing—no cars, no refrigerators, no expensive toys—but they were happy because they had each other. They had the love of family and the support of their community." As I listened to Zac's response, watching the candlelight play across his young face, my eyes filled with tears.

For a young man who had lived a life of privilege yet had suffered from depression, this was a revelation.

Like Singita, Mombo Camp was a luxurious and expensive accommodation; while we hadn't discussed much about our respective backgrounds, it was clear that visitors to this camp were typically people of strong financial means. So each person at that table immediately understood the import of Zac's observation. And the response was reverent silence.

After the meal, several of the guests congratulated me on what a wonderful young man I had raised. Once Zac returned to our cabin and the rest of us gathered around the after-dinner campfire, several of the remaining guests—with surprising emotion—expressed their appreciation for the beautiful lesson he had taught all of us on that quiet and dark jungle evening.

As I wiped the tears from my own cheeks, I marveled that here in Africa, thousands of miles from our affluent communities, God could speak to me and to the other guests through the observations of an eighteen-year-old boy—an eighteen-year-old boy who was rapidly becoming a man.

·············· *For Reflection* ··············

I am not saying this because I am in need, for I have learned to be content whatever the circumstances. I know what it is to be in need, and I know what it is to have plenty. I have learned the secret of being content in any and every situation, whether well fed or hungry, whether living in plenty or in want. I can do all this through him who gives me strength.

Philippians 4:11–13

• •

When children of wealthy families who live in very affluent communities struggle unsuccessfully to meet the lofty demands and expectations of their parents, resulting failures can cause many to become seriously depressed and to self-medicate with alcohol or drugs. Sadly, the resulting downward spiral—one that is difficult to escape—often leads to suicide. Thankfully God can help break that cycle by revealing the values that really matter. That's exactly what happened on my trip to Africa with my eighteen-year-old son, Zachary.

Have there been poignant moments in your life or in the lives of your family members when suddenly you saw God in others who were ostensibly less fortunate than you? Have you witnessed the unbridled joy and contentment of those who seem to possess little and want for even less? If you can recall such experiences, try to remember how they impacted you and your attitude toward life. We are often inspired and motivated by people who have overcome major obstacles and have in the process experienced a closer relationship with God and a deep appreciation for life. May God help us find ways to learn the secret of being content in any and every situation as Paul expressed in his letter from prison to the Philippians.

Chapter 3 Exercises

Chapter 3 recounted experiences in which God dramatically intervened at various crossroads to guide me (and others) down the right course. At any one of these critical moments or decision points, the consequences and the course of the future could have been quite negative. Certainly many people will attribute good choices and outcomes to luck. But as one who has a strong faith and relies daily on God's loving and gracious guidance, I firmly believe that the spirit of God dwells within me and, at times, reacts and responds quickly to a crisis or the need for an immediate decision.

God to the Rescue

The most dramatic instance of this guidance occurred when I was a young boy about to take a ride with my dad—when that small voice within warned me of danger and told me to check behind the car only to find a sleeping infant directly under the rear wheels.

- There certainly have been experiences in your life that you later looked back on and said to yourself, "Oh, how my life would have been different if this or that had or had not happened." Try to identify one such event that ultimately resulted in a positive outcome.
- Try to recall and describe the circumstances surrounding that event and how your life today would have been different, if it hadn't happened.
- By exploring the ways your life developed after that pivotal event, ask yourself whether this might have been an intervention by God after all.

Workplace Intervention

Throughout my career, I brought God into the workplace. I prayed to Him and relied on guidance from the Holy Spirit every day of my working life. I had the blessed assurance that He was with me and guiding me throughout my career. But there were particular crossroads I faced during my career when God provided the necessary guidance through the voices and actions of others. In the story "A Career Turning Point," God spoke to me through the candid and thoughtful feedback of my mentor and boss, Jules Pallone. His timely advice and constructive criticism put me on the right path.

- Do you believe God is with you in the workplace? Are you seeking His guidance and direction daily at work?
- Can you recall a time when you felt God was in control of your response to a difficult situation, especially one with which you had previously struggled unsuccessfully?
- What were the circumstances of the event? What approaches had you considered in dealing with the issue? Describe what God's divine solution looked like and the ultimate outcome.

Touching Troubled Hearts

At an important crossroad in his life, my son Zac, who was struggling with the emotional devastation of clinical depression, made life-altering observations on a trip we took to Africa. In the story "Lessons for the Affluent in Africa," it was God who revealed these lessons not only to Zac but to me and the other unsuspecting guests during a moonlight dinner at Mombo Camp in Botswana. With the realization that true happiness doesn't depend on material possessions, all of us were given a new perspective.

- Do you consider yourself a "happy" person?
- What is it in your life that contributes most to that happiness?
- How can that realization affect the way you live your life from this day forward?
- How can you transfer that awareness and wisdom to others?

Chapter 4

GOD REVEALED . . .

ACCORDING TO HIS TIMING

Like many people, I often pray and hope for—even expect—almost immediate answers to my yearnings . . . only to learn that answers don't come on my timetable. God's responses to many needs seem to be either nonexistent or significantly delayed.

However, in God's infinite wisdom, His timing is unfailing. Sometimes it is years later that things we have prayed for actually materialize. In other cases, God knows what we need to shape our future, to fortify our faith, or even to advance our careers. His reinforcing messages may come with incredible timing even when we haven't explicitly prayed for anything. In my view, those providential experiences of exquisite timing can only have come from a God who knows us and knows what prodding, encouragement, or nurturing we need at a particular juncture in our lives.

God's perfect timing is the theme of the following stories. I hope they will trigger your memories—times when your needs (whether you prayed about them or not) were separated by months or years from an event that later seemed to address them. And if you make such a discovery from your past, think about actions you can take now or in the future to be more attuned to God's providential nurturing. Ask yourself why the prayers went unanswered for so long and how the final answer may indeed be in God's perfect timing.

The Miracles of Childbirth and Adoption

Even before our marriage, Sue and I shared a love of children and a strong desire to raise a family. We had both enjoyed very happy, traditional childhoods in two-parent families in the lower-middle-class suburbs of Detroit and were eager to provide similar experiences to our own children. Our love for children also led both of us to pursue teaching-related careers during the first few years of our marriage.

Unfortunately, we were unable to conceive a child. It is difficult to fully express the emotional distress of realizing that one may never have children after so eagerly anticipating the joy of parenthood. Devastated, we embarked on several years of medical testing, fertility treatments, and praying.

It has been my habit to pray many times a day throughout my adult life. God has always been there for me and I was (and am) confident that even though I don't hear an audible response, God is guiding my actions. So even though we were worried and disappointed, we trusted God to bless us with children. And although we knew that God responds on an appropriate timetable, we were discouraged as the years continued to pass without a baby.

We lived in Detroit, and for several years I had been going across town to Dr. Robert Leach at a clinic in Beaumont Hospital for testing and fertility treatments. After having no success in increasing my sperm count through hormone injections, he and I agreed to discontinue treatments. Even though my count was extremely low, another fertility specialist recommended by Dr. Leach convinced us to try in vitro fertilization using my own sperm.

Those attempts also met with failure, and I reluctantly resigned myself to the reality that I would never father children of my own, and I plodded through the months of dejection and depression that followed. Agreeing with Dr. Leach to "give up" my infertility testing and treatment was doubly troubling for me as a Christian: Was I giving up on God? And was God giving up on me?

Finally we made the decision to try in vitro fertilization with donor sperm. Sue and I both struggled with this decision as it meant accepting an unknown father to my children. We had always planned to adopt children, so the thought of having children conceived with a donor's sperm was not completely objectionable. But was this God's will? Or simply a convenient rationalization?

Even with a donor's sperm, all attempts at conception again failed, and Sue and I were ultimately told by numerous doctors that neither of us would ever produce children. My sperm count was almost nonexistent, and Sue could not conceive even after several attempts at in vitro.

Even more depressed, we began the effort to adopt. The process was tedious with lengthy applications, medical exams and references, and visits and interviews by social workers that all seemed highly bureaucratic and time-consuming. There was also significant cost, legal work, and required documentation.

However, over many months the depression finally abated as we began to anticipate the presence of an adopted child in our home, and our excitement mounted as we prepared for our Korean daughter Heidi. The thought of providing a loving home for a baby who was abandoned in a basket on the steps of a church in Seoul, Korea, filled us with joy; the arduous process was well worth the effort.

In a year or so, the joys we experienced in raising Heidi not only allowed us to recover from our depression over infertility but also encouraged us to initiate the adoption process once again. In 1979, we received Dena, a five-month-old Korean who had been given up for adoption by an unwed mother from a rural village outside Seoul. How blessed we felt by our growing and beautiful young family after so many failed attempts at conceiving a child.

The adoptions of Heidi and Dena were followed by a local adoption in Michigan in 1983 of a special-needs infant, Denise, at age two and a half. Denise was special in many ways, and she came to us unexpectedly with only a few days' notice. A social worker contacted us to ask if we would consider adopting Denise immediately to remove her from a difficult foster home environment. We visited her on a Tuesday afternoon and felt led by God to welcome her into our home on Saturday of the same week.

How happy we were raising our girls and enjoying the lives of a typical young family. The stress and depression over our infertility were long forgotten when a miracle occurred. After sixteen years of marriage and three adoptions, God blessed us with Sue's pregnancy and the birth of Zachary in 1986. The joy and wonder over this gift from God is difficult to put into words. There was no question in our minds that God had finally answered our prayers but in His perfect timing, not ours.

And a short eighteen months later, along came the miracle of the birth of our second son, Corey. Thanks to God's miraculous gifts, our household was suddenly and unexpectedly bustling with the sounds and activities associated with raising two infant boys. Our daughters loved being big sisters and though we worried about their reaction to natural-born brothers, we never saw any evidence that they felt like second-class members of the family. Love and joy were seen and felt in abundance.

Ironically, after these rapid-fire miracles, Sue and I had to face the prospect that our newly found fertility could create a major financial challenge and, a very short five weeks after Corey's birth, along came the miracle of a vasectomy! We concluded that five children were quite enough and wanted to make sure another little miracle didn't surprise us.

When we made the decision that I would undergo a vasectomy, my physician referred me to a urologist at a small clinic associated with Beaumont Hospital. When I looked up the urologist's name and address, I once again thanked God for not only divine influence but also a divine message. Detroit is a huge metropolitan area with hundreds of local clinics and medical specialists. Yet of all these, the urologist to whom I had been referred was located on the same floor in the same medical building as Dr. Leach, the fertility doctor who had unsuccessfully treated me so many years before.

My eyes filled with tears of remorse as I realized that in that very clinic I had given up hope of ever conceiving a child. Dr. Leach and I had given up on medical science, and I had given up on God. I viewed this uncanny "coincidence" of place as a reminder from God that the births of Zachary and Corey were true miracles and answers to prayer. God had heard my prayers, and long after we had given up hope, God remembered us and answered those prayers—in His own *divine* time.

On the day of the vasectomy, although I was quite nervous about the procedure, I was excited over the thought of finding Dr. Leach to tell him the purpose of my appointment. He remembered me, and I watched excitedly for his reaction as I told him I was there to have, of all things, a vasectomy after the totally unplanned and unanticipated natural conception of two sons in rapid succession.

After a few long seconds of speechless, wide-eyed amazement, he congratulated me and without further comment returned to his patients. How odd that Dr. Leach didn't say much in response to our miracle; maybe he wasn't ready to admit that he had failed where only God could succeed. Perhaps I was not the first such patient for whom prayer had accomplished the seemingly impossible.

As I look back on our history, I firmly believe that the real blessing in this story was not the birth of the boys, but rather the temporary infertility. The infertility triggered our efforts to adopt. Perhaps the message was to trust God to answer prayer on an appropriately divine timetable and in His way.

Sue and I are reminded and thank God daily for the blessings of the births of our boys and the adoptions of our girls as we interact with our five beautiful children and our two grandchildren. God has given us the family we dreamed of in those early years of marriage, and we are grateful for and humbled by the greatness of that gift.

·············· *For Reflection* ···············

Yet this I call to mind and therefore I have hope: Because of the Lord's great love we are not consumed, for his compassions never fail. They are new every morning; great is your faithfulness. I say to myself, "The Lord is my portion; therefore I will wait for him." The Lord is good to those whose hope is in him, to the one who seeks him; it is good to wait quietly for the salvation of the Lord.

Lamentations 3:21–26

· ·

If you're like me, you pray often. Consequent to that, you hope for—and sometimes expect—almost immediate answers. But, in my experience, the answers don't always come, and they rarely come on my timetable. After years of unsuccessful fertility treatments, I gave up on God but He had something far more glorious in store for us and He answered our prayers in His perfect timing.

In my view, those providential experiences of exquisite timing can come only from a God who knows us and knows what prodding, encouragement, or nurturing we need at that particular juncture in our lives.

I believe in miracles, and I believe God still performs miracles every day. I also realize that many times we don't get an immediate response from God, and the miracle we seek doesn't occur when we think it should or in the way we desire. But God has a way of giving us so much more than we ever expect, and my repeated experience has demonstrated that His wisdom and love always result in an ultimate outcome that is to our greatest benefit.

Have there been times in your life when you reached out to God in prayer but felt your prayers went unheard or unanswered? As you think back on those experiences and on subsequent events, do you now better understand God's timing and His ultimate response to your supplication? Were the answers to your prayers simply deferred, or were they possibly manifested in a completely different way than what you had anticipated? Can you see and admit in retrospect that God had it right, and that perhaps, at the time, you simply weren't being patient and waiting for the Lord?

Maybe you are praying right now for a miraculous healing, for the resolution of a long-standing personal conflict, or for help with one of the other serious issues we all face in our imperfect human existence. Perhaps you haven't yet had an answer to your prayers—at least not in the way you have hoped. If so, don't be discouraged. In my case, ultimately God transformed what I perceived to be unanswered prayers about infertility into the unexpected blessing of the marvelous gift of a large, happy family. Continue to seek God's will. As you do, your strength will be renewed as you wait for the Lord and His perfect timing.

The poems of Lamentations encouraged the faithful to wait on the Lord even in the aftermath of the tragic destruction of Jerusalem by the Babylonians, who had laid waste to their homes, families, and God's temple. And yet, in the face of the greatest of calamities, in the midst of mourning the losses of the people and even despairing of the future, the author pauses to call to mind God's great love and compassion. It is this one thought—a reflection on the faithfulness and mercy of God—that brings him hope. Although my faith and hope waned in the face of my infertility, and my discouragement and impatience caused me to effectively "give up" on the Lord, I am now ever mindful that His compassions never fail and that it is good to wait quietly for the salvation of the Lord.

A Posthumous Business Lesson from Dad

Just prior to my dad's death in 1994, my career was somewhat uncertain. I was a relatively new executive vice-president at New York Life Insurance Company, hired from the outside into a conservative organization that much preferred to promote from within. I came to the company with a hard-driving management style that was much more focused on aggressively tackling problems and achieving ambitious objectives than on celebrating successes. I had a well-deserved reputation of setting unrealistic expectations and micro-managing employees without giving recognition to, or expressing appreciation for, achievements.

To use a medical metaphor, I found myself frequently concerned that the corporation would ultimately reject me as an unwelcomed foreign substance within the body corporate.

It was in this emotional state of vocational apprehension that I faced the experience of bidding farewell to my much-loved father. Our entire family was driving home from Michigan to Connecticut after an emotional and spiritually awe-inspiring two-week visit with my ailing father when we received the call telling us he had passed away. The news was not unexpected; just days earlier he had experienced a near-death transcendence into the world beyond (which I'll explain in a later story), and he had been eagerly awaiting his own final passage. His subsequent testimony to us about the love and bright beauty of the other side had given us hope and courage, feelings that helped to ease us through the news of his passing.

We still had over 100 miles to go to return to our home in Connecticut and there was an eerie silence in the car for the remaining two hours of that trip. All that could be heard from my five children was an occasional sob and some sniffling as they remembered Grandpa and fought back tears. My eyes watered as I worked hard at paying attention to my driving. It was difficult.

But in that moment of grief, I felt Dad and my love for him. My mind ricocheted back over decades of images: Dad working so hard day and night for his family; Dad playing the trumpet professionally in the evenings; Dad working! And suddenly I realized that Dad was the source of my work ethic.

The images of Dad kept coming, and as we got closer to home and the traffic got heavier, it became increasingly difficult to concentrate on my driving. It was dangerous, but it was impossible to control the images. Our family meant everything to Dad, and he worked very hard to make life as comfortable as possible for Mom, my brother, and me. How much he had sacrificed for us, with so little time for leisure activity or even for family vacations. Our one family vacation flashed into my mind— images of Dad trying desperately to pretend he could be an outdoorsman and knew how to fish.

More and more, the memories rushed in: Dad attending sporting events to watch his two boys play—something that gave him joy but, at times, also caused family discord, as his expectation of strong athletic and academic performance was more often perceived as demanding than encouraging. This too was a trait I unknowingly took from Dad. It was my M.O. in the workplace.

During that drive, I thanked God for giving me many rapid-fire and pleasant flashbacks of my years with Dad. Those years went by so quickly, and I didn't tell Dad often enough how much I loved and appreciated him. Having these recollections was an experience that I thought of as a gift from God, helping me to deal with the grief of my loss.

Despite my distracted driving, we finally arrived safely at home— where we almost immediately unpacked, repacked, and arranged to fly back to Michigan to deal with the funeral arrangements.

Back in Michigan, cloistered in Dad's basement, going through boxes and boxes of personal papers in the days before and after his funeral, I came across a green hanging file containing handwritten notes he'd received while working as an insurance inspector many years earlier. These short, simple expressions of appreciation from his superiors were often nothing more than a handwritten message that said something like, "Fred—nice job on this case." Alone with my thoughts, my emotions again overtook me as I thought of Dad's humanness. He was never a manager of people; he was a working employee at the bottom of the organizational chart. How much these small gestures of appreciation from his superiors must have meant to him!

I read and reread many of the short notes. How easy and meaningful a simple expression of praise or appreciation could be. And how much such an expression could mean to an employee at any level. Dad had saved these notes over many years and had probably reviewed them often during his retirement.

I was managing New York Life's largest business unit, one that consisted of more than 10,000 agents and 4,000 employees. Only eight or ten executives reported directly to me, but I knew hundreds of employees and agents personally. How infrequently I had thanked them for a job well done or had expressed encouragement. Dad was at the bottom of his company's organizational chart and I was at the top of mine. Sitting in his basement among scattered boxes of papers and that small green file, I was overtaken by a sense of guilt and lost opportunity. How could I be so driven and not understand the human need for recognition, appreciation, and encouragement? This was a moment from God. I needed this lesson desperately and it was delivered by God, indirectly by Dad, through the documents he left behind.

On the same day that I discovered my dad's file of notes, I came face to face with my past. I was taking a break from the tedious work in the basement and, still in awe over the lesson I had just learned, I drove to the nearest shopping mall. Walking through the mall, I noticed a man who looked very familiar.

"Are you Fred Sievert?" he asked.

"Yes," I answered, instantly recognizing him. It was Alan Lauer, an employee who had worked for me many years earlier when I was an executive at Maccabees Mutual Life Insurance Company in Southfield, Michigan. It was wonderful to see him.

"Fred," he said pounding me on the shoulder. "Fred Sievert! I still remember when you called me after a presentation I made to our executive management committee. Do you remember that?"

I confessed I did not.

"During that call, you told me how much you appreciated my work and how confident you were in my knowledge and abilities," he told me. Then he went on to say that my call had meant a great deal to him and that it had caused him, a relatively new employee, to conclude that he had chosen the right position at the right company that had the right leadership.

What a wonderful and reassuring message for me to hear. And how incredibly remarkable that it occurred only hours after I had discovered Dad's file of complimentary notes and felt remorse over my present-day lack of appreciation.

This could not have been a coincidence. It was just too timely and too improbable. Dozens of times over the years, we had returned to Michigan to visit family and friends and I had been in that same mall on nearly every trip. Never once had I seen anyone I knew. Thank you, Lord, for reminding me of that simple management tip and of how easy it is to overlook.

As a result of this revelation, I started a practice the following Christmas season of sending annual holiday greeting cards to more than 300 New York Life employees. In each card I included a handwritten personal note of appreciation for that person's work on behalf of the company over the prior year. Since this was a time-consuming task, I started the process well before Thanksgiving each year.

Years later, at a number of retirement parties held for me throughout the country and even around the globe, many people thanked me and told me what those cards meant to them. Many, including my successor as president, even indicated that they had saved a file of their cards. How moving it was to hear that my employees were replicating my dad's practice—but this time those files contained messages from me. Another posthumous gift from Dad!

·············· *For Reflection* ··············
Do not let any unwholesome talk come out of your mouths,
but only what is helpful for building others up according to
their needs, that it may benefit those who listen.

Ephesians 4:29

···

Our behaviors and the words we use to express ourselves to our family, friends, and colleagues at work can have a powerful and lasting effect on those individuals and our relationships with them. Our actions and our words can have either a very positive effect or a devastatingly negative one. In the above excerpt from Paul's letter to the Ephesians, his primary admonition seems to be against "unwholesome talk," but don't miss in his message the emphasis on "building others up" in a way that will "benefit those who listen."

As my career was advancing in the mid-1990s, I needed to be reminded of the impact of my demanding management behaviors. My drive, ambition, sense of urgency, and strong work ethic often caused me to be perceived as domineering and unappreciative of the excellent efforts and results being produced by those who reported to me. A change was needed, and little did I realize at the time how God would lead me to accomplish that change.

As in so many of life's experiences, when chance encounters extend beyond mere coincidence, it's likely that God is orchestrating the events and delivering a message. That's how I interpret what happened to me in 1994.

Think about those improbable coincidences that have occurred in your life, significantly altering the course of your future. What could have happened if what you learned or experienced through those events had not occurred? Try to imagine how your life may have been worse without that divine lesson. My lesson from Dad was really a lesson from God delivered through the papers Dad left behind and the highly improbable meeting with a former employee in a shopping mall on that same day. The lesson for me ultimately was about expressing appreciation and giving encouragement, something I was woefully neglectful of before Dad's death. God knew where I was failing, and He delivered guidance in a way that was timely and undeniable.

Encouragement and expressions of appreciation can impact relationships in all of our human interactions. My lack of attentiveness to this simple practice in dealing with subordinates in the workplace is only one such example, but there are many. How do you treat your friends, your parents, your siblings, your spouse, your children, or other members of your family? Have you developed a habit of expressing encouragement and appreciation to the important people in your life? Or have you been too often guilty of tearing them down rather than building them up?

God may not have smacked you between the eyes with a clear and undeniable message like He did me, but please learn from His providential message to me as you reflect on your own past practices. Remember: as Paul suggests in Ephesians 4:29, use words that build up and benefit those who listen.

Unexpected Lessons from President Clinton

New York Life was the sole sponsor of the PBS series on the U.S. presidents that premiered on public television in 2000. My leadership position at New York Life at the time gave me the opportunity to meet many of the past presidents as well as the incumbent president, Bill Clinton.

To launch the series, the White House hosted a small event; in addition to some of the actors, actresses, and producers of the series, five or six top New York Life executives and directors were invited. I had been to other White House events over the years, so this was not new, but this would be the first time I would speak with an incumbent president.

The series launched only months after President Clinton's impeachment hearings following his admitted sexual relationship with twenty-two-year-old White House intern, Monica Lewinsky. Like many Americans, I found Clinton's behavior upsetting. A fifty-two-year-old married man having sex with a twenty-two-year-old girl was objectionable enough, but, to me, it was inexcusable for the leader of the modern world to become such a negative role model for the youth of the nation. Nonetheless, I sensed there was something for me to learn about the mystery of human behavior through interaction with a highly successful and brilliant man who had allowed himself to succumb to such temptation.

After passing through the tight security of the White House, we walked up a long stairway lined with large portraits of former presidents; a small uniformed military band at the top of the stairs provided patriotic music. From there we walked into a grand ballroom positioned between the East and West Wings where we were served drinks and hors d'oeuvres as we awaited the arrival of the president.

About ten minutes before the president was due to arrive, I moved to the back of the room, where I could get an expansive view of the back lawn. There, on the putting green behind the White House, was President Clinton dressed in a jogging suit, a golf putter in hand. He walked among dozens of golf balls strewn across the green, stopping at each one and putting it toward the single cup in the center of the green.

At the time, I was aggressively climbing the corporate ladder, often working more than fourteen hours a day. With little exercise and only four or five hours of sleep a night, not only was I neglecting my family but also my physical and mental health. Even on our annual vacations, I usually got up at 4 a.m. to review and answer email messages and to delegate assignments to my staff. I was in a high-level corporate role with significant responsibilities, I had a great deal on my mind, and I almost never took time to read the newspaper or anything other than insurance industry trade journals.

Watching President Clinton wandering around on that putting green, most certainly clearing his mind of a huge number of pressing issues and difficult pending decisions was stunning: here was the most powerful man in the world—a man who had recently gone through some embarrassing and highly public hearings, investigations, and interviews—taking time to clear his mind by putting golf balls while dozens of guests awaited his arrival.

If the president of the United States could take quiet private time to relax and refresh, why couldn't I? Why was I neglecting my family and my personal health for a far less demanding job than his? I looked out the window again in time to see one of the president's assistants walk onto the green, evidently to tell him it was time to come in and get ready for the evening's event. The president took two or three parting putts before he exited the green and walked through a back entrance.

Unbeknownst to him, the president had just given me a valuable lesson. And the more I thought about my position in comparison to his, the more I suspected that this evening would indeed be meaningful and memorable.

Twenty minutes later we were escorted into the West Wing, where a hundred or more folding chairs were set up in front of a presidential podium with a projection screen behind it. President Clinton arrived shortly and shook a few hands as he sat down in the front row. A White House official introduced New York Life Chairman Sy Sternberg, who made brief remarks about New York Life's sponsorship of the series, introduced a few short video clips, and then introduced the president.

President Clinton delivered a very informative thirty-minute presentation (with no notes) about interesting historical events that had occurred in the White House and about many notable decisions that had been made in the very rooms we had visited that evening. Like most Americans, I had heard the president speak many times in televised news coverage, but to sit a few feet from him and observe the ease with which he articulated his remarks was to watch a true master at work. I was very impressed with his knowledge of prior presidencies and the key events that had shaped our history as a nation.

Following the president's remarks, our small group was invited to a reception in the East Room where an elaborate buffet was set up with enough food to feed twice as many people. As we mingled, President Clinton walked around the room, stopping to speak with all of the guests either in small groups or in one-on-one conversations. He stopped and spoke to me and my wife, Sue, for nearly fifteen minutes.

Prior to this evening, I had been told by many people that President Clinton was an incredible conversationalist. We now witnessed the truth of that. He focused intently on our conversation and made us feel as though we were the only people in the room. He was charming, charismatic, and remarkably attentive and responsive to everything we said. In fact, we were enjoying ourselves so much and feeling so comfortable in his presence that we both nearly forgot about the Lewinsky scandal and his most recent travails.

We discussed New York Life, its key business strategies, and one of the officers at New York Life whom we had hired away from her White House position to assist us in expanding our international operations.

"So you're the guy who stole Sandy Kristoff from me," said the president, jokingly pointing his finger at me. Then he told us that Sandy was one of his most trusted employees because she always told him what he needed to know instead of what he wanted to hear.

Wow. How many times had I reacted negatively to unanticipated "bad news" rather than seeing it as honest and necessary information?

How furious I'd been when poor financial results were revealed to me by the accountants and actuaries well after it was too late to take corrective actions. What hadn't occurred to me until this minute was that I'd learned the news late because I'd repeatedly discouraged early disclosure with my negative reactions; some feared that I might "shoot the messenger." What President Clinton said made total sense and how I now regretted never having had this new perspective. Well, it was never too late to change. From that point forward, I would use the expression, "Tell me what I need to know, not what I want to hear."

I knew the president didn't realize he had given me a wonderful personal lesson on the putting green—and that now, just as casually and perhaps just as unconsciously, he had provided me with an important leadership lesson. So I was silently grateful.

As our conversation turned to a discussion about the emerging New York Life business in India, it became instantly clear that President Clinton felt great passion for India—both for its people and for their circumstances, including poverty, poor infrastructure, and poor water quality. He spoke highly of India's potential for economic growth, the industriousness and ambition of its people, and the potential for him to be personally involved with them following his term in office.

As Sue and I listened—listened deeply with interest and appreciation—something amazing happened: Our disdain for his immoral behavior evaporated. His compassion for the underprivileged in India was sincere. This man had a good heart and was truly committed to serving and helping others.

And this brought the third lesson of the evening: If a man as busy as the president of the United States demonstrated compassion for the underprivileged, and that compassion had caused him to develop his post-retirement plans early, I could certainly do the same. Although I'd already considered taking an early retirement, in my constant busyness, I hadn't taken the time to consider what passions I'd follow and what meaningful purpose my life would serve. The discussion with Clinton caused me to search my soul and initiate an extensive planning exercise for those areas of passion that I would pursue when I left New York Life.

My experience that night had already been richly imbued with lessons. But the last lesson of the evening was perhaps the most important and included a powerful message from God.

In our final couple of minutes with President Clinton, I mentioned how impressed I was with his earlier presentation. He told me he had taken a strong personal interest in history and that he was particularly interested in determining why each president was the right man for the job at that particular moment in history. It almost sounded as if he felt God had ordained each presidency.

In light of these comments, my last question was obvious: "Mr. President," I said, "how do you view your presidency in that regard?"

His answer surprised me: "I was the right man for the job at this particular time, because who else could tolerate what they've put me through?"

Inwardly I chafed at his reference to the extensive negative press coverage of a number of alleged scandals during his presidency, culminating in the most recent Lewinsky situation. But out of deference for the office of the president, I bit my tongue and didn't ask the next obvious question: *What do you mean what THEY put YOU through?* Why couldn't he take full responsibility for his precipitous behavior with a twenty-two-year-old White House intern instead of considering himself the victim?

But even in that low moment, I had a strong, positive feeling, and it was perhaps the most important lesson of all: We all possess the God-given free will to behave as we choose. God has given us the wonder and beauty of the physical pleasures we enjoy in a committed relationship. Those physical desires can easily be channeled in an inappropriate way, and the associated temptations are no respecter of class, rank, or economic status. In fact, the opportunities for such behaviors are most certainly far greater for individuals with power, and they may be even more tempting for those living intensely stressful lives.

My own sins may have been different than Clinton's but I had recognized myself as a sinner many years before and truly believed I was saved by God's grace. Why didn't I remember that as I had so inappropriately passed judgment on Bill Clinton?

Finally, through the guiding of the Holy Spirit, I saw his humanity and felt compassion for him. He was as fallible as the rest of us—a reminder to me of the importance of always being on guard against life's inappropriate temptations. For the very first time, I was able to forgive Bill Clinton, and I felt grateful for the profound lessons he had taught me that day.

·············· *For Reflection* ··············

Get rid of all bitterness, rage and anger, brawling and slander, along with every form of malice. Be kind and compassionate to one another, forgiving each other, Just as in Christ God forgave you.

Ephesians 4:31–32

···

When we put the past behind us with genuine forgiveness, we often rediscover what we may have failed to see as a result of our own self-righteous attitudes: the goodness of friends and loved ones. In his letter to the Ephesians, the apostle Paul exhorted the people to effectively "bury the hatchet" and move forward in forgiveness and with God's love. Forgiving others as God in Christ has forgiven us can be very difficult when we feel we have been wronged, especially when our forgiveness must be unilateral and unconditional.

Sometimes we feel betrayed or harmed in a societal sense instead of in a direct, personal way. It's very easy to be critical of the behavior of others, particularly those in high-ranking positions of authority like President Clinton. In such cases, we still need to forgive as God has forgiven.

Forgiveness may not come naturally to many of us as we harbor ill feelings toward those who have behaved badly, even if their behaviors do not directly impact us. Nonetheless, even if forgiveness is not verbally communicated—and therefore is not appreciated or reciprocated—it can have a therapeutic and beneficial impact on those of us who consciously forgive.

Are you harboring resentment toward someone you once considered a close friend? Do you feel you have been wronged or betrayed by a family member or a previously cherished friend, and do you find that you simply can't let go of those negative feelings? Or perhaps, as in the same way I reacted to President Clinton, you feel betrayed or wronged by someone in a position of authority? That person could be a superior at work, or it could be someone who has authority over decisions that impact the members of your family, your local community, your state, or even your nation.

If your anger and resentment is toward a close acquaintance or a family member, remind yourself of what originally attracted you to that person and why that relationship remains important to you. Maybe you have family ties or common interests or simply share a natural rapport. Perhaps you don't want to admit that you are partially responsible for the estrangement that has resulted. I encourage you to forgive that person and commit to putting the past behind you. Reach out to God with prayers for guidance, and then reach out to the individual to seek reconciliation.

You may find that such efforts still fail to resolve an issue with someone who is unwilling to engage with you on the matter or, worse, refuses to acknowledge the problem exists. A good example is a family member who is an abuser or who suffers from substance addiction. Forgiveness becomes especially difficult in these situations but you may find that reliance on prayer and God's own example of divine forgiveness will sustain you.

On the other hand, your indignation or outrage may have resulted from the misconduct, iniquity, or injustice of a person of authority with whom you have little or no direct contact. If so, you may have to forgive completely on your own—your forgiveness may need to be unilateral and unconditional.

Regardless of the circumstance, experience the sweet and freeing emotions that come with forgiveness by following Paul's exhortations in Ephesians 4:32: "Be kind and compassionate to one another, forgiving each other, just as in Christ God forgave you."

The Hanoi Hilton: Burying the Painful Past

During my presidency at New York Life, I often made visits to Washington to lobby issues of particular interest to the company and the insurance industry. These visits were typically intensely busy with very few breaks. I'd arrive on an early-morning flight and meet first with the New York Life government affairs staff for a briefing on the day's schedule and the most important issues on the legislative agenda. There followed multiple meetings with members of Congress in fifteen- to twenty-minute sessions throughout the remainder of the day. There was no break for lunch, and my last meeting finished just in time to hail a cab to the airport, where I caught a shuttle flight back to LaGuardia.

In 1999 and 2000, New York Life was expanding its international operations and was eager to obtain licenses to sell its products in the huge, underpenetrated insurance markets of India and China. In exchange for China's rapid consideration of our license application (which otherwise could take many years to process), we had agreed to lobby on their behalf in the United States for Permanent Normal Trade Relations (PNTR), something that would facilitate their rapid acceptance into the World Trade Organization (WTO).

My visit to Washington this day in 2000 was to lobby in support of the PNTR bill for China, which was scheduled to come to a vote in the House of Representatives in May.

The day began with several early meetings. Then, as I hurried to a late-morning appointment with Congressman Sam Johnson of Texas, a Vietnam vet and former POW, I received the usual mobile briefing from our on-site Washington government relations officer, Jessie Colgate. She told me about Congressman Johnson's long history in the House, his voting record on similar issues, and the basic nature and characteristics of his constituents in Texas. We also talked about the market share of New York Life in his district and how we could best argue for support of the PNTR bill for China. It was as thorough as a briefing could be in a fast-paced twenty-minute walk from one building to another. But there was one more thing, and as we approached Sam Johnson's office, Jessie got nervous. "Fred, you should know Sam was a prisoner of war at the infamous Hanoi Hilton in Vietnam for almost seven years," she said.

China was an ally of North Vietnam during the war and provided military supplies and support to the North Vietnamese.

"I'm afraid Sam harbors negative views of the Chinese," she continued. "He's likely to debate any proposal to support Permanent Normal Trade Relations with China."

I knew atrocities sanctioned by national authorities can generate lasting feelings of enmity against an entire country—its people, its customs, and even its cultural production. Evidently Sam's long-standing hostility against his captors and torturers would likely extend to an entire nation of people who had little or nothing to do with his pain and suffering more than thirty years earlier.

We arrived a couple of minutes early to the meeting, so Jessie and I discussed what I might be able to say, and I became increasingly anxious. On one hand, I felt honored to be in the presence of a great American who had given so much for his country and had sacrificed so greatly. But on the other hand, I knew I was likely to face some strong and passionate resistance to my proposal.

Taking a deep breath, I entered Sam's office and announced my arrival to his receptionist, who asked me to take a seat in the typical congressional office waiting area: small and modest, with one couch and a chair; the walls were lined with photographs of the congressman posing with numerous political leaders. One that caught my eye was a nicely framed formal commendation from the House of Representatives that recognized Sam for his exemplary service in Vietnam. On the plaque was a quote from a North Vietnamese official saying that Sam Johnson was one captured American soldier they could not break.

What an astonishing statement. I was awed by the obvious loyalty and courage of this great American patriot. Would I have had the courage to withhold information under intense interrogation and torture?

As was usual for such meetings, I still didn't know for sure if I'd be seeing Sam or a representative from his staff, and I'm embarrassed to say that for a moment I actually hoped he wouldn't show up. But if he did, maybe I'd simply talk briefly about New York Life, thank him for his service to the country, and leave without ever raising the PNTR issue. How nervous I was as I sat in the waiting area . . . gradually and uncomfortably flooding with guilt, my normally low heart rate and blood pressure escalating.

It's in moments like these that I believe God speaks to me through my emotional and sometimes physical reaction to my own thoughts. As my nervous system went into overdrive, I sensed that God was calling me a coward. Clearly, my plan to escape this confrontation was not worthy of the courage and dignity of the man I was about to meet. Certainly it would be uncomfortable to raise the PNTR issue with the congressman, but I suddenly realized that my discomfort couldn't begin to compare to the torture he had endured for his country. I had to face the challenge. I had to step up to the task.

Finally I was escorted into Sam's office, and I was somewhat stunned and saddened as he slowly walked toward me with a noticeable limp—certainly related to the torture. And when I shook his big hand, I was equally moved by what felt more like a beanbag than a firm Texas handshake. The North Vietnamese probably broke the bones in his hands in their attempt to extract information. Later I read the following on his website about his service in Vietnam:

During his second tour of duty, Johnson flew his 25th combat mission on April 16, 1966. Shot down at dusk over North Vietnam, Johnson suffered a broken right arm, dislocated left shoulder, and a broken back. It was these injuries that the enemy captors would use in their constant efforts to glean information from Johnson.

Johnson spent nearly seven years as a prisoner of war, 42 months in solitary confinement. He was forced into solitary confinement when his captors labeled him a "die-hard." While held in the infamous Hanoi Hilton, Johnson spent 72 days in leg stocks. A day after that torture ended, his captors forced him into leg irons for 2 1/2 years. Weighing 200 pounds when shot down, an emaciated Johnson got down to an estimated 120 pounds while barely surviving on the occasional "meal" of weeds from the river, pig fat, white rice, or pumpkin soup.

Fellow POW Captain James Mulligan, USN (ret.), recalled the day Johnson was allowed to return to a joint cell. He walked into the room with the two other detained American officers, "stood at attention with tears in his eyes, and said simply, 'Lieutenant Colonel Sam Johnson reporting for duty . . . sir.'"

As we sat down and exchanged pleasantries, my nervousness was somewhat replaced by gratitude. I thanked God for the opportunity to meet Sam and for my marvel at America's long history of courageous heroes.

Following a ten-minute summary about New York Life and our important strategy of exporting our expertise to international markets as we expanded globally, I quoted some quick statistics that pointed to the tremendous opportunity in many Asian markets and then, as my nervousness returned, I began to go through my talking points in favor of PNTR for China.

Instantly, Sam stopped my pitch. "Why on earth would New York Life want to do business in that country?" he asked, frowning and squirming in his chair.

I explained about China's massive market of more than a billion people, its rapidly growing economy, and the need for life insurance, which to date was not readily available to people in China.

Again he interrupted. "Do you really think this is an environment in which you could grow and sustain your business?" He pointed out the many well-publicized reports of difficulties other companies had recently experienced with the Chinese, alleging that in China there was little respect for intellectual property and an eagerness among their domestic companies (and even the government) to learn from and then apply foreign companies' knowledge and expertise. He also alluded to the concerns of many Americans and others regarding China's spotty record in the area of human rights.

I responded the best I could, increasingly frustrated as I realized my efforts were likely futile. Moreover, I didn't want to offend or antagonize a man who had suffered so much at the hands of a military organization closely aligned with the Chinese.

It was then that I believe that God entered the discourse by providing me with an instantaneous, unplanned inspiration and a way to touch Sam more personally.

"My daughter Dena recently spent a semester abroad in China," I told him. "She is a devout Christian who attended Calvin College, a Christian school in Grand Rapids, Michigan. During her semester in China—you're right—she witnessed censorship and oppression relative to religious worship, but she also made many friends and was able to share her faith."

With courage that could have been inspired only by God, I suggested to Sam that if we as a country continued to avoid interactions with the Chinese, we would miss an opportunity to share our values and our faith. If we refused to open the dialogue, we would probably continue to see cultural misunderstandings and wouldn't even have an opportunity to impact human rights. "But by providing permanent normal trade relations for China, we stand a far better chance of generating not only expanded trade and commerce, but also the exchange of cultural ideas and values," I said.

Sam listened, and then responded, his argumentative tone transformed into one that was more contemplative. I wasn't sure if he was simply politely ending the debate or if he really was beginning to soften. Bidding him good-bye, I hoped and prayed that I had been duly respectful in my discussion and that, despite his painful memories, Sam would thoughtfully consider our position toward the China bill.

A few days later I enjoyed one of the most gratifying moments of my career when Jessie Colgate called me. "You'll never believe this," she said. "Congressman Sam Johnson voted in favor of the PNTR for China bill!" She congratulated me and asked how on earth I had managed to convince him.

I deserved none of the credit, I told her; it was God's work in bringing us together, providing the words I uttered about my daughter's experience and softening Sam's heart to the current realities about a nation largely disconnected from his painful past. In God's perfect timing, all things are indeed possible and good can overcome evil.

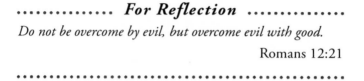

·············· *For Reflection* ··············

Do not be overcome by evil, but overcome evil with good.

Romans 12:21

The apostle Paul closes this chapter of his letter to the Romans by summing up how Christians must respond to evil, particularly to evil enemies. Rather than responding to evil with more evil, we should overcome evil with good.

History is marred by nearly continuous periods of war and strife; the rare periods of world peace are fleeting and difficult to identify. The willingness of humans to inflict extreme pain and suffering on other humans has been demonstrated repeatedly in examples of genocide and claims of "just wars." In the face of such pain, suffering, and loss of life, we struggle to convince ourselves that God is alive and intervening on our behalf. One of the single most difficult theological questions is why God allows such suffering—and the absence of a logical and credible answer to that dilemma provides significant fuel for atheism and agnosticism.

Equally difficult to comprehend is the use of torture against captured enemies in an effort to secure classified information. Despite such atrocities, I maintain my faith and occasionally see glimpses of healing, propitiation, and forgiveness. During my divinely timed exchange with a true American military hero—Congressman Sam Johnson—God gave me a glimpse of how one man's long-standing hatred of an oppressive nation and its operatives can ultimately be reconciled.

Think about experiences when you have been bullied, persecuted, or grievously wronged. Your feelings of hatred and anger are only natural and may persist to this day, years after the event. You may even be estranged from family members, former friends, or other acquaintances. If such is the case, please use this example of Sam Johnson's extreme circumstances to ask yourself if forgiving and putting those differences behind you could free yourself of such negative feelings—and could help you reconcile your differences and move forward in a positive way. Congressman Johnson found it difficult to forgive the heinous crimes against him—and, as is a natural human tendency, he even extended responsibility for such crimes to an entire nation and its people, even though they were, at the very most, only distantly connected to that dreadful past. Yet, as painful as that history was, Congressman Johnson was able to see a different future, one ready to make room for goodness.

Let God speak to you about these situations. As you exhibit God's unconditional love and grace to others, you may experience an incredible blessing yourself. As Paul suggested in Romans 12:21, rather than harbor ill will and remain estranged for decades, seek reconciliation and forgiveness and "overcome evil with good."

Chapter 4 Exercises

Chapter 4 retold situations in which I experienced God's perfect timing—timing that often didn't meet my desires or match my expectations. I hope that the brief exercises below will allow you to resurface examples in your past of times when God provided instantly what you urgently needed as well as examples of when God delayed His answers. There may even be examples of prayers that you feel went unheard and unanswered. I think we can learn from thoughtfully revisiting those situations and attempting, in hindsight, to understand why God knew, and acted upon, what was best for us.

Divine Intervention

God was there instantly for me as I responded to arguments and objections raised by Congressman Sam Johnson. Can you think of examples in your life in which God was there for you precisely at the moment when you needed Him most; when the timing was exquisite?

- Describe the situation. Were you praying for God's guidance or did it come unexpectedly?
- At that instant, were you aware of God's intervention? How did you respond emotionally?
- Did your experience reveal more to you about the nature of God? If so, in what way?

Answers Deferred

Despite our persistent prayers, the birth of our two biological sons, Zac and Corey, didn't occur until we had been married for more than sixteen years. The wisdom and blessing of that timing only became clear to us after the joys of adopting our three daughters, Heidi, Dena, and Denise. Think back on your life and try to identify some of your prayers that went unanswered for a long time but eventually were answered in God's timing.

- Describe the situation and how long you prayed and waited.
- Did you feel that God had ignored you? Did this challenge your faith? If so, how?
- How do you believe God ultimately answered those prayers?
- Does your experience support the claim that God answers in His perfect timing?

Unanswered Prayer?

Undoubtedly, there have been times when all of us felt God ignored or abandoned us. Perhaps we had an urgent need and prayed for God's intervention to no avail. Did God really hear our prayers and, if so, did He ignore them? Within the limitations of our mortal minds, we don't always find plausible answers to these difficult questions. Do you have examples of prayers that seemingly went unheard and were never answered?

- Provide an example of a situation in which you appealed to God in fervent prayer but never (or at least have not yet) received an answer?
- Do you still pray and hope for an answer to those prayers?
- In hindsight, can you now think of reasons why God's answer may have been "no" or "not yet"?
- Has your faith wavered as a result of this experience?
- Does listening to the stories of others with similar examples help you to better understand your own situation and why God's timetable may not match yours?

Chapter 5

GOD REVEALED . . .

IN OUR HOURS OF NEED

W hen God intervenes on our behalf to answer prayers or perform miracles, we are not likely to forget those experiences. It should be easy for you to recall miracles that you have witnessed as you reached out to God in desperation or in extreme adversity. I encourage you to identify the miracles in your life—even those that don't seem as striking—and to hold all of them dear as you continue to rely on God for guidance.

The stories in this chapter are very personal and speak to divine interventions in my life and in the lives of my family members. If they trigger memories of similarly important times in your life, I invite you to tell others your experiences. Your future as well as the future of the people you tell will most certainly be enriched.

Doing What's Right

At age five in 1953, I lived in a small, quiet Detroit neighborhood. This was before the advent of the now-ubiquitous prekindergarten programs, and preschoolers ruled the neighborhood while the older kids were away at school during the day. Because there was little fear of crime or kidnapping and because we lived on a short dead-end street, even the four- and five-year-olds had a lot of freedom to wander. I played with my friends all morning and afternoon with a noontime break for lunch either at my house or at a friend's.

Dads were home from the war, most moms worked at home raising their children, the post-war economy was booming, and there was a sense of security and hope from which even young children could benefit—if only through the happiness and prosperity of their parents. We almost never went anywhere in the car, nor did we eat at fast-food restaurants very often. We were allowed to watch our small black-and-white television set—with its rabbit-ear antenna that picked up only a weak and fuzzy signal—for limited amounts of time. There was no Internet, no computers, no calculators, no cell phones, no iPods, no PlayStations, and no Twitter or Facebook. We made our own fun, and somehow we survived without electronic assistance.

There were many more street vendors and retail delivery trucks than we see in residential neighborhoods today. Nearly every day the milkman made his dairy product deliveries, a paperboy tossed newspapers on the porches, and the ice-cream truck wound through the streets in the late afternoon or early evening. Others, such as produce vendors or locksmiths, came through periodically. Traveling salesmen walked door-to-door selling everything from encyclopedias and vacuum cleaners to brushes and other household items.

As young kids in the neighborhood, we got to know these salespeople, many of whom became quite friendly with us and sometimes offered us small, inexpensive gifts. Those entrepreneurs who worked our neighborhood often seemed like extended family to us and to our families.

I connected especially well with our milkman, who drove a small truck into the neighborhood every day. He usually came very early, but sometimes I saw him as I went out to play after breakfast. "Hey, Freddy," he called to me one day. "How would you like a ride in my truck?"

This was an offer I couldn't refuse, so I quickly jumped into the front seat, with open doorways on both sides to expedite deliveries. The last thing I remember from that ride was the truck rounding a corner—and me losing my grip and falling out. Though I couldn't remember any of it, I was thrown from the truck and knocked completely unconscious when my head struck the curb.

Was I dead? Had I suffered serious brain damage? The milkman, the neighbors, and my mother feared the worst.

While I was unconscious, my parents—who up to that time had never taken me to church and had only rarely expressed belief in God—prayed intently for my full recovery.

When I finally woke up, I was in a hospital room with my parents at my bedside. "Oh, Fred!" cried my mother, grasping my father's hands. "Oh, Freddy! Thank God! Thank you, God!"

And from that time forward, I heard more about the goodness of God and divine answers to prayer—a topic that was somewhat foreign to me as a five-year-old, but it planted a seed.

Despite my regaining consciousness, the doctors remained guarded in their optimism for my full recovery, and I stayed in the hospital for a couple of days under observation; subsequent tests were performed regularly, and prayers continued indefinitely. How scared I was in the large dormitory-like hospital room with seven or eight adult patients. But after those few fearful and uncertain days, I returned home with a clean bill of health.

And home became slightly different. We began attending church only occasionally, but talk of God was much more evident than it had been before the accident. And after I completely recovered, my parents told me that we were going to visit somebody—an attorney who would ask me about what had happened to me.

"Hi, Freddy," he said. "I hear you got a big bump on the head. Can you tell me about that?" He seemed like a nice man; he treated me gently, but for every answer, there was a more probing question: "What can you tell me about that ride?" "Did the milkman give you and your friends rides often?" "Were you scared?" It was like he was trying to get me to say bad things about my friend.

After I nervously answered his questions, my parents were encouraged to sue the dairy company for negligence because the driver had allowed a five-year-old to ride on one of the milk trucks. How much money a judgment or settlement might yield—I didn't know, and as a child, I wouldn't have understood such figures anyway.

"No, we are not going to do this," said my father, resolutely. "But thank you very much for your guidance."

At that time, my family was really struggling to make ends meet, and I now realize how difficult it must have been for my parents to resist that enticing temptation.

Later on, they carefully explained it to me: "The milkman made a terrible mistake, Freddy. He never should have offered a ride to someone as young as you." They emphasized that I could have been killed or could have incurred permanent brain damage. "Because of that," they told me, "we could have been paid a lot of money for the company's mistake and for the continuing risk to your health."

I was too young to understand the intricacies of lawsuits, but I asked a lot of questions. "I don't get it," I said. "Why don't you want the money?"

"Try to understand, Freddy," said my mother. "We are so grateful that God returned you to us and healed you. He answered our prayers and will protect you from harm in the future. So even though the lawyer said to take the money, we feel that it's better to forgive the milkman and the company and not to seek any further gain from the accident."

I finally understood: Their decision was a conscious display of gratitude to God for my healing. They felt strongly that this was the right decision—the right thing to do—and that God would bless our family in the future, providing for their financial needs, for making that decision.

It occurs to me now how infrequently children get to witness meaningful and practical applications of faith, particularly on the part of their parents. I suspect many (if not most) children who are far better churched and Sunday school-educated than I never get such a clear and unambiguous example of faith in action as I did at the age of five.

The right thing to do is an expression I would subsequently revisit hundreds of times in my personal and business life. Just as my parents believed He would, God did bless our family, and I thank God often for the wonderful and lasting life lesson my parents taught me.

.... *For Reflection* ....
Start children off on the way they should go, and even when they are old they will not turn from it.

Proverbs 22:6

....

God doesn't always intervene to prevent accidental deaths, even among faithful believers. I don't understand why, but I have confidence and faith that all things work for good in the lives of those who believe in and follow the Lord our God. In my own life I was extremely blessed following the childhood accident that could have easily killed me: God protected me and granted me a full recovery. Perhaps just as valuable as that blessing was the valuable life lesson I learned through the faith and the actions of my parents.

Children are incredibly impressionable in their formative years. We often forget that they are always watching our actions and behaviors and listening to our words. Whether they like what they hear and see or not, we are their role models. It's undeniable that both our positive and negative behaviors as parents are frequently mirrored years later in the behaviors of our adult children. The high frequency of abused children later becoming abusers of their own children is but one clear example.

Moral behaviors, the values of parents, and the training of children are all extraordinarily important in your children's preadolescent years. Even if they reject or rebel against parental morals and values in their adolescent or teenage years (a very common occurrence), most ultimately revert to the role models and examples set for them in their formative years. Do you see your parents' behaviors reflected in your own actions? Can you separate the good from the bad and work to consciously avoid negative behaviors modeled by your parents?

Are you a positive role model for your children? Are you bringing them up in the way of the Lord? The Proverbs are so rich in wisdom. There is no greater truth than the counsel of Proverbs 22:6 to start children off on the way they should go, because—as the scripture promises—ultimately they will not turn from it.

Prayers for Mom

In 1980—when I was thirty-two and my mother, Rose, was sixty-two—my parents were living in Michigan. Three years earlier in 1977, after much prayer and consideration, Sue and I had moved to the Boston area so I could start a new career. It was a particularly difficult move, as we were leaving both of our parents and taking their two-year-old granddaughter away from them. Now we had two young Korean daughters: Heidi, age five, and Dena, age two.

It was a cool and otherwise lovely New England autumn morning when I received the call from my father. "Freddy," he said, in a soft and faltering voice, "I want you to know that Mom was experiencing chest pains and dizziness yesterday so I took her to the hospital and she was admitted for testing. The results showed significant arterial blockages and she has now been slated for surgery as soon as possible."

Sue and I were hit hard—not only because my mother's life was at stake but because we lived so far away. Also, we'd never faced the reality of our parents' mortality at such a young age, and we'd assumed we had many years left to visit.

The hours that followed were tense, to say the least. Suddenly consumed by the realization that I hadn't told my mother often enough how much I loved her and how much she meant to my personal and professional development, I longed to talk to her. I had so much to say—about my faith, about her incredible influence during our numerous kitchen-table talks throughout my youth, adolescence, and early adulthood. Her encouragement and persistent advice to always act with integrity had shaped my life and had tremendous impact. Thank God there was still time.

"Freddy," said my father over the phone on the day of her surgery. "You need to know the truth. The doctor said there are significant risks for someone with such major blockages. Okay?"

"Okay," I said, completely rattled. All I could do was hold fast to my faith in God—and a hope that His will would mesh with my own.

"Okay, then," said Dad. "I'm going to put your mother on."

I fought back the tears as we spoke. I wanted to demonstrate my faith in God and my courage in the face of this dangerous surgical procedure but I couldn't shake off the realization that, if it was God's will, I might never see her again—might never again enjoy the wisdom of her advice during our kitchen-table talks or feel the warmth of her loving hugs. I told her—for what I realized might be the last time—how much I loved her and appreciated her considerable efforts in raising me. "I'll be praying for you, Mom," I reminded her. "After all, miracles happen and all things are possible for those who believe and trust in God."

Then I covered the mouthpiece to muffle my sobs as she told me how proud she was of me, my young family, and my professional accomplishments.

I believe in the power of prayer because I believe in a living God who hears and answers prayers. I also understand that those answers aren't always on our preferred timetable or what we would desire but rather are on God's timetable and according to God's will. Like many Christian families, we did not pray often enough together as a family. But this was clearly one of those moments when we were frightened and in desperate need of divine intervention.

Later that morning—the morning of Mom's surgery in Michigan—Sue, Heidi, Dena, and I were driving to a local shopping mall in Walpole, Massachusetts. After I parked the car in the mall parking lot, we prayed together not only for successful surgery but also for a complete healing of Mom's condition. The prayer lasted no longer than a minute or two. Sue and I fought tears as we finished and considered the possibility of a less-than-satisfactory outcome. Nonetheless, we trusted that God's will would prevail.

Later that day my father called to report the results of the surgery. "You're not gonna believe this, Freddy," he said, clearly amazed. "The doctors didn't even believe it. They performed the exploratory surgery and found clean arteries! As clean and clear as a newborn baby's!" Dad recounted what the surgeon had told him: no matter how successful subsequent surgery might have been, the arteries never could have been restored to this condition—yet it had happened before any surgery was performed. "Her surgeon said it had to be the result of divine intervention!"

To say we were grateful is an understatement.

For the rest of her life, Mom required no surgery. Despite having a very poor family health history—her father, mother, and brother all died at very young ages—she lived to the age of eighty-three, when she quietly and peacefully died in her sleep in April 2001.

Following her miraculous healing in 1980, we enjoyed many more years together as well as many more loving hugs and encouraging kitchen-table chats. After what we experienced in 1980, it was natural to share our faith much more often. It was also much easier to frequently express our gratitude to God for giving her more than two additional decades to enjoy her children and grandchildren during her mortal existence.

················ *For Reflection* ···············
Again, truly I tell you that if two of you on earth agree about anything they ask for, it will be done for them by my Father in heaven. For where two or three gather in my name, there am I with them.

Matthew 18:19-20

··

Many times it takes a crisis to bring us to our knees before our God. Too often we wait and call out to God as a last resort. I plead guilty to that charge. My family had prayed together far too infrequently—but my mother's condition and surgery frightened us as we were confronted with the real possibility of losing her so young.

Throughout my life I have heard others tell stories of miraculous healings. I've often wondered whether they were real miracles or simply the outcome of advanced medical science. I must admit to earlier episodes of testing God by praying intently for the healing of an obvious physical affliction—such as blindness—in which the healing would be immediately evident. I believed then, as I do now, that all things are possible through a living, loving, omnipotent God, but I should have known better than to test Him in that way.

In my estimation, my mother's healing is incontrovertible proof of God's healing power and God's daily presence in our lives. Her heart was restored to its youthful condition *before* the surgeons opened her chest cavity.

Can you recall any similar miracles in your life? Have you either long forgotten those experiences or, worse, have you somehow rationalized them away as luck? Be reassured and inspired by the significant probability that God had a hand in saving you or a loved one. Honor Him by retelling your story of that miracle in a way that will inspire others. I am constantly mindful of the power of prayer, particularly when we join our hearts and souls with fellow Christians to make our needs known to God in the name of Jesus Christ. Make a habit of speaking to God daily and gather with others to do so as Jesus tells us in Matthew 18:20.

The Migraine Headache Cure

Since early adolescence, I suffered from classic migraine headaches. Doctors believe that migraine headaches are most commonly stress-related, though they are often triggered by external stimuli. In my case it seemed that most often my migraines were triggered by bright lights: the glare of the sun off of water or the glare of bright lamplight shining on a highly reflective surface, such as the pages of a magazine or a recently waxed and polished linoleum floor.

I and many others who suffer from migraines experience an *aura*, an early warning sign before a severe headache develops. When the auras occur I feel no pain—just slight dizziness or light-headedness and uncomfortable but painless pinpoints of light that lead to spot blindness. For many years, my reaction to this disconcerting loss of sight was to close my eyes, a response more psychologically satisfying than functional.

To the best of my recollection, my first headache occurred during puberty when I reacted to the glare of a bright reading light reflecting off the surface of a glossy magazine cover. It was absolutely terrifying to sense that I was losing my sight. I found through experimentation that if I could get to sleep before the extreme headache developed and could remain asleep for five or six hours, I would awaken with a severe pounding headache that was painful but far more tolerable than a full-blown migraine. Moreover, I would awaken with my vision restored.

If I could not "sleep it off," the ensuing headache rendered me totally debilitated for at least two days. During that time I became even more sensitive to light and had to remain in as dark a room as possible. Once the headache emerged, I also experienced sound sensitivity; everyone in the house had to remain totally quiet. For many hours after the onset of a full-blown migraine, I was in excruciating pain and could not stop vomiting, even long after there was nothing in my stomach. Occasionally the dry heaving resulted in bleeding.

In that miserable state it was impossible for me to leave my room. As a result, I missed a couple of days of school two or three times every year during my youth. The condition persisted through junior high school, high school, and college. When I began teaching in 1971, I always had back-up lesson plans ready to use in the event a migraine surfaced. Once a headache was in progress, there was no way I could put together and deliver lesson plans to the school before the pain became unbearable.

Over the years, I sought medical treatments, consulting with several different physicians and specialists to no avail. Even the brain scans and hormone and allergy testing were inconclusive and simply resulted in the same diagnosis: classic migraines. I was given various pain-killers to minimize the pain of the headache, but even if I could hold down the medication without vomiting (which was not usually the case), the pain-killers had very little impact.

While teaching in the early 1970s, I needed to find summer employment to supplement my meager income. Another teacher who for many years was employed as a Greyhound bus driver during the summer months put in a good word for me, and for the next five summers I too was driving for Greyhound Bus Lines. I was constantly on call, and because of heavy travel in the summers, I worked the maximum hours allowed by federal transportation laws. I often had only minimal rest periods between trips.

I typically had two hours' notice to appear at the Greyhound garage in Detroit for an assignment that could last as long as ten hours. At the end of those ten hours, Greyhound was required to give me eight hours' rest and another two hours' notice before the next assignment. This insane work schedule continued around the clock from the end of June until after Labor Day, when school began. It was a hectic pace, but supplemented my income nicely.

I rarely knew where I'd be traveling until I reported to the Greyhound garage, so I always carried a small suitcase with a change of uniform and toiletries. Out-of-town sleeping arrangements were far from ideal; I usually slept in a drivers' dormitory with multiple beds in a room, I shared bathroom facilities, and the constant smell of diesel fuel filled the air. I occasionally enjoyed a private sleeping room about the size of a jail cell with no windows and a single overhead light bulb.

During the five summers I worked for Greyhound, there were two or three occasions when I rejected a driving assignment at the last minute because of an emerging migraine headache in its early aura stage. My short notice gave dispatchers too little lead time to find a substitute driver, and each time I was given a written reprimand and a stern scolding from management. I'm not sure the managers believed me, and I feared I would lose my job if it happened more than once each summer.

One warm summer evening I was asked to be at the drivers' room in Detroit by 10 p.m. I hadn't had much sleep but dutifully arrived at the appointed hour and learned my assignment: the late-night run to Louisville, Kentucky, from 11 p.m. until 7 a.m. It was a long haul, I was tired, and there was only one brief rest stop in Findlay, Ohio, at about the halfway point.

For the first two hours of the trip, everything went well: The thirty or more passengers slept and I felt fine. But suddenly things changed as I began to sense the onset of the migraine aura. I was an hour away from the rest stop and faced three or four more hours of driving after that. Spot-blindness would make the second half of the trip dangerous at best and impossible at worst. *Oh God*, I thought, *before we reach Louisville I'll have a full-blown headache complete with extreme light and sound sensitivity and nonstop vomiting.*

When we arrived at the rest stop in Findlay, the spot-blindness was becoming very noticeable. Should I request a replacement driver? It would cause a huge delay for the passengers and, given my personnel record, I'd most certainly be fired.

Cautiously I made my way into the small cafeteria at the rest stop and searched for the bathroom. The blindness was so pronounced that I had difficulty determining which restroom was for men. Fairly certain that I'd chosen correctly, I entered, walked into one of the stalls, and got down on my knees to pray. The prayer was short and simple: "Heavenly Father, in the name of Jesus, help me to know what to do in this situation." After talking to God, I immediately sensed and concluded that I should take my chances and drive through to Louisville.

Thinking ahead to the very real possibility that I might be vomiting uncontrollably before arriving in Louisville, I found some bags at the rest stop that could serve as "barf" bags. My contingency plan was to claim a bout of the flu or food poisoning to excuse my sickness; by continuing to drive, I hoped to demonstrate how committed Greyhound drivers were to delivering passengers on time to their intended destinations.

I knew I had made a very risky decision that could even result in injury to the passengers. But I trusted in God to get us safely to Louisville.

As I returned to the freeway, I was experiencing major pockets of blindness. I couldn't read any of the road signs, but the remainder of the route was entirely freeway driving and there was very little traffic on the freeway at 3 a.m. I straddled the white line between lanes to make sure I didn't run off the road and awaken the sleeping passengers. I was very anxious about the onset of full-blown pain and nausea but I was prepared for that eventuality and was determined to make it to Louisville without losing any passengers or my lucrative summer job.

In the next few hours something truly remarkable happened. As I continued my drive to Louisville, my vision gradually cleared. I braced myself for the extreme light sensitivity, sound sensitivity, nausea, and excruciatingly painful headache, but none of that occurred. I dropped off the passengers in Louisville and drove myself to the dormitory, free of symptoms and perplexed. For the first time in my life, the aura had not been followed by the predictable progression of symptoms. I was euphoric. Not only that, but after bedding down in the drivers' dormitory, I was shocked and amazed to awaken six or seven hours later feeling rested, refreshed, and physically energized. And I thanked God for bringing me safely to Louisville and for miraculously preventing the symptoms that would have left me trapped for two or more days in the dormitory until I totally recovered.

It occurred to me that God wanted me to learn from this experience, so I began to consider what had been different this time from all of my prior migraine episodes. On the bus, I had been forced to stare through the blindness instead of closing my eyes to it. I took no medication. And because I was driving, I couldn't lie down and try to "sleep it off."

Ever since that day in 1975, my response to an aura is very simple. No matter what time of the day or night, I stare through the spot-blindness, take no medication, and make no attempt to sleep until after the temporary blindness disappears. The aura still occurs three or four times a year—and has done so consistently over the past thirty-five years—but by following my simple plan I have not experienced a single migraine headache.

So that night in the bus in 1975, I was effectively cured of a debilitating illness. I attribute this cure to God. Being able to avoid such pain has not only made me happier but has also made me more productive and successful in both my business and personal life.

I have mentioned my simple discovery to a number of physicians and have also sent my story to a medical journal. I subsequently received mail from several people who read my story and applied the same technique, resulting in similar relief from their own classic migraines.

It gratifies me greatly that God was not only speaking to and curing me, but also enabling me to positively impact the lives of others who found relief from pain and suffering by reading my story.

.... *For Reflection* ....
Cast all your anxiety on him because he cares for you.

1 Peter 5:7

Thanks to the marvelous miracle that occurred when I was in my mid-twenties, I no longer suffer the excruciating pain and debilitating aftereffects of migraine headaches. God was there listening to me and responding as I bowed my head and clasped my hands in an empty toilet stall at 3 a.m. in the men's room of a freeway rest stop in Findlay, Ohio.

Not only did He guide me instantly to the right decision, but He also provided an answer to an urgent and abbreviated prayer in a way that would produce lifelong relief. Ever since that day, I have made it a regular practice to seek God's advice, guidance, and healing power in short but earnest prayers multiple times daily. It's not an exaggeration to say that throughout my business career I offered up succinct appeals to God ten or more times daily as I faced difficult decisions. It is also true that the answers are not always forthcoming. In those situations, bolstered by my strong faith, I try to understand why the outcome may be different from what I desired. It is His will and not mine that concerns me the most, and I need often to remind myself of that fact.

It occurs to me now that I may have missed an even greater message from God in finding the cure to my migraines. Perhaps my migraine "solution" applies to other areas in my life. "Staring through the blindness" may be a metaphor for confronting life's challenges, and not "sleeping it off" relates to our natural tendency to hide or escape from our biggest problems. Having the courage to face those challenges coupled with reliance in God through prayer is the real "cure" He was revealing to me.

Do you reach out to God in prayer as you face life's inevitable challenges? Can you think of examples when God's response was almost instantaneous? If so, be a blessing and a beacon of hope to others by sharing that experience. Perhaps there's even a greater message than you thought—one that will apply to other people's problems.

Have there been other occasions when you felt God let you down or abandoned you? In hindsight, do you now understand why the timing may have been wrong? If so, you should also share your insights on those experiences—reasons for unanswered prayer can be helpful to others whose faith may be wavering as they seem alone and are finding it difficult to understand God's timing.

Whatever the circumstances, I would echo Paul's advice in 1 Peter 5:7: "Cast all your anxiety on him because he cares for you."

Dad's Transcendence

Death is an integral part of life, and each of us will eventually face the loss of a loved one. But at the age of forty-six, I hadn't yet experienced the death of an immediate family member. When we moved our family of seven to Connecticut in 1992, I was very concerned over the deteriorating health of my father; he was diagnosed with cancer shortly after our move.

I am grateful that in August of 1994 my entire family was on vacation in Michigan for two weeks and we had a chance to express our love and our faith to Dad before he was gone. I will never forget my sixteen-year-old daughter, Dena, telling Dad to remember, "Jesus is real. And Jesus loves you."

In the middle of that two-week period, Dad slipped into a coma. For several hours, he lay staring with his eyes open but with no eye movement, and we finally left fully expecting to receive news during the night that he had died. To our surprise, there was no call.

Dad not only survived the night, but when we returned to the hospital the next day, he was sitting up eating his lunch, more alert and energized than he had been in weeks. The nurses told us they couldn't believe his good spirits and how dramatically he had changed overnight. He was visited earlier that morning by a long-time friend, and the two of them enjoyed a wonderful reunion.

Amazed to see him so alert and lucid, I asked what he recalled of his condition the day before. To me he'd looked like he had already died. Perhaps he'd been having a near-death experience similar to those I had read about and heard others speak of. I'd given such stories little credibility. Dad was not a religious man—certainly not one to share his faith outwardly—but he was a good and honest man of faith who worked tirelessly to support his family and always tried to live by righteous principles. If anything had happened, I knew he would give an accurate and earnest account according to his best recollection.

"I saw a wonderful, loving world! It's a beautiful place, Freddy, beyond description, and I can't wait to return," he said with glee. While he was in the coma, he had an encounter he had often heard of and read about. "I was drawn into a beautiful and warm bright light. In the warmth of that light, all of my pain slipped away and I was completely immersed in goodness and love." Naturally, he wanted to return; in fact, he had derived his renewed energy and spirit from the fact that he'd be returning there soon. Dad was tired and didn't elaborate much further. He never said he saw Jesus, but this was clearly a transitional moment for him—a truly transcendent and ecstatic experience.

When we said our good-byes in the hospice a few days later and started our drive back to Connecticut, I was surprised that, even though we all knew we would not see my father again in this life, I wasn't sad. It wasn't until I thought about the events that had transpired that I recognized why sorrow was not on my radar screen.

After Dad's experience, we all realized that we could look forward to a reunion with him in the life beyond. I was so grateful that I had been with Dad for those final two weeks and that my dismay over his comatose state had turned to joy when I learned he had been given a peaceful and inviting glimpse of the world beyond. We left feeling we had just had an experience blessed by God, who had actually revealed divine truth to Dad and to the family through him.

We were very close to our home in Connecticut when I received the call that Dad had died. It was the first major loss of a loved one in my life, yet it didn't cause agonizing grief or pain. God had watched out for my family in allowing us to arrive before Dad died. If he had died two weeks sooner, I would not have heard my daughter's confession of faith to him, I would not have heard the story of his near-death experience, I would not have shared in his glimpse of the blessings of the other side, and I would not have had the personal reassurance of the gift of eternity provided by a gracious and loving God. I will forever be grateful for each of those gifts.

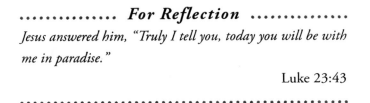

.... *For Reflection* *..............*
*Jesus answered him, "Truly I tell you, today you will be with
me in paradise."*

Luke 23:43

We often read of near-death experiences. Perhaps some of us discount them as illusions or hallucinations. That all changes when someone close to us—someone we trust and believe unequivocally—has such an experience. That's what happened to me at the deathbed of my father, and it was an experience that enriched my life immeasurably. What an incredible blessing that before my father died, God would provide reassurances of an eternal existence that relieved my fears and comforted my soul. Since then, I have recounted my father's transcendence to many friends and acquaintances only to learn that near-death visions and experiences are far more common than I realized.

Have you had such an experience, or has anyone you trust ever related such an experience to you? Have you ever conducted a deathbed vigil with a loved one until the moment at which he or she passed to the life beyond? If you have, you probably recall the last words or facial expression as he or she ascended from this life to the next.

I take comfort and joy in knowing that I will indeed be with Jesus in a glorious "paradise" as He promised in Luke 23:43.

Chapter 5 Exercises

Chapter 5 tells stories of what I found to be undeniable miracles. God's healing powers for potentially fatal illnesses were revealed in physical cures that went well beyond even what I asked for in prayer. If you have had similar miracles in your life—whether you recognized God's role when the miracles happened or in hindsight—you now have a story to tell that can positively impact many other lives.

Rewarding the Faithful

Even though my parents were not strong worshipping Christians, they had an unfailing belief in God and taught me important moral lessons from the time I was very young. In the story "Doing What's Right," they resisted the temptation to pursue a lawsuit after I was seriously injured in an avoidable accident. They did so despite the insistence of lawyers and the potential for financial gain. They did so because they were grateful to God for my recovery and believed God would continue to bless the family as they faced continuing economic challenges. They were right!

- Can you think of a time that your parent's or guardian's actions provided you with a similar life lesson?
- If you are a parent or guardian, have you had the opportunity to demonstrate to your children your faith and your moral values through your own actions and words?
- Do you believe God rewards righteousness?

God's Healing Power

Perhaps the most dramatic example of a miracle was the cleansing of my mother's blocked arteries just before she was to undergo heart surgery. As told in the story "Prayers for Mom," our pleas were granted and the results were confirmed as the doctors opened her up to find the pristine-like condition of her arteries. Certainly many such prayers go out daily and many people believe their prayers are unheard and unanswered. I don't know why some prayer requests seem to be denied, but I trust that God hears all such prayers and there are reasons for the ultimate outcomes. However, I do know when prayer requests are dramatically and miraculously granted, and my mother's healing was one such case that I am blessed to reveal to others.

- Do you believe God hears and answers prayers in His wisdom and according to His will and timing?
- Have you ever personally experienced or seen evidence of God's healing power? If so, describe the miracle.
- On the other hand, when there is no immediate miracle— for instance, when you gather together in groups to pray for healing for friends and family and those prayer requests seem to be denied—in what ways have you dealt with that experience? Did it test or diminish your faith?
- Have you found it possible to reconcile the sorrow that comes from seemingly unanswered prayers with what you know of God's biblical promises?

Glimpses of Eternity

It's only natural for people to be skeptical of reported near-death experiences. But when someone we know and trust relates such a story, we give it credence. In 1994, only days before he passed away, my father awakened from a coma just long enough to relate a glorious near-death experience to me and my family. And even though his ultimate death was my first loss of a close family member, the grieving process was dramatically truncated and less difficult knowing that he had had a glimpse of heaven and was eager to return. It was indeed comforting to have the assurance that he was beyond his earthly pain and suffering and experiencing the joy and happiness of eternal bliss.

- Have you or anyone close to you ever had a similar experience?
- How do you reconcile differences in the descriptions of these experiences when they are had by different people?
- Many people return to altered lives after such an experience. Why do you think God takes some into His glory while returning others to their mortal existence?

Chapter 6

GOD REVEALED . . .

IN OUR FAMILY RELATIONSHIPS

Who among us does not see God in the attachment to our own parents, in the miracle of childbirth, in the love we have for our family, and in the glorious experiences we share with those so close to us? Much of my spiritual growth and most of the important messages and revelations I've received from God have come through family experiences and interactions. God has revealed Himself to me many times in incredible family experiences that reminded me not only of my blessings but also of my responsibilities. I have highlighted here five particularly poignant stories of family experiences that generated unforgettable and lasting joy—experiences that were embraced by God and infused with His love.

As you read my stories, think about your own family times and traditions. If you aren't already tuned in to the messages God has sent you through your family, try listening carefully for what God is telling you through your interactions with close family members. For instance, I am certain those of you with children or grandchildren will find it easy to recall moments when the love of God manifested itself in the warmth of cherished family relationships and experiences. It may be that you have felt God's presence in the faithfulness and support of a beloved brother or sister. Or perhaps yours is a story of finding family along the way, not by blood, but by God's love and grace.

Searching my memory banks for earlier messages has been a richly rewarding experience, and I am convinced that your future will be enriched if you too can recognize, anticipate, and even create more opportunities to experience the love of the family God has given you.

Memories of Mom

Parenting is a blessed responsibility, and I grieve for those who either don't recognize its immense importance or, even worse, abuse its sanctity. As I look back on the ways God has spoken to me through my family relationships, my memories of my mother's love and nurturing come readily to mind. My mother, Rose Sievert, was perhaps the greatest contributor to my happiness and fulfillment, in both my personal and business life. I have many enduring memories of her, but two stand out.

The first happened in my grandfather's home, the very home where Mom had been raised. I was five years old. Most children will sleep in their parents' bed at one time or another, but I remember it happening only once. My mom and I were staying overnight at my grandfather's small home in Detroit. A Polish immigrant of very modest means, my grandfather raised a son and three daughters while working hard as a manual laborer in an automobile factory; his home was small with a tiny guest bedroom, which my mother and I were to share that evening. The only bed in the guest room was twin-sized, so we were close throughout the night. But it went far beyond a physical closeness; I remember my emotional response as vividly as if it happened yesterday.

My mother held me and kept me warm from the very cool breeze coming in through the open window. I remember the strength of her heartbeat against my little arm, which was wrapped around her, and I recall thinking that she would always be there to protect me and care for me. I remember waking in the morning with her still holding me tightly as if she'd never let me go. And I can still recall the fresh smell of the recent rainfall and the sweet sound of the bird that was singing to the rising sun. Life was so simple and safe then.

That experience was a gift from God—a part of His grand design. It was the most important bonding experience I have ever had, and it was the first time I was conscious of my physical and emotional response to true, unconditional, and embodied parental love. As I think back now on the impact of that single experience, I begin to realize the truth expressed by so many psychologists and psychiatrists: Maternal Love in one's formative years is crucial, as is hugging and providing other expressions of love to our children. How unfortunate it would be to be deprived of such love—and worse, how devastating it would be to experience physical or emotional abuse from one's own mother or father.

As I grew older, I could feel the force of that same love in everything my mother did and said. Throughout my adult life, Mom continued to nurture and support me in good times and bad, through various joys and challenges. She was always there to protect and care for me, and she continued to love me unconditionally.

The second memory of my mother that had such impact is something that happened many times in the common setting of a simple kitchen table. I had literally hundreds of conversations with Mom during our private times there, which we fondly called our "kitchen-table talks." She always told me how much she loved me, how smart I was, and how someday I would "make a difference" in the world. She talked about life's challenges and how important it was to be true to my values and always do what was "right." I could go on at great length about these conversations, but her underlying message was, *You can become whatever you want to become—just don't do it in an unethical or immoral way.* Her coaching and encouragement centered around two recurring themes: *self-esteem* and *integrity.*

Ironically, although God or religion didn't come up often in those discussions, a lot of moral principles she shared became embedded in my psyche. Throughout my childhood and even into adulthood, Mom always emphasized that I could accomplish anything as long as I worked hard and did so with integrity. Although those chats were never formal Bible studies, she often quoted the Ten Commandments and the "Golden Rule" as ways in which I should live my life. I believed her. I listened and always heeded her advice, which was given out of that great love and protection that I had felt so vividly as a young child.

In the decades that followed those childhood experiences, whenever I was faced with difficult personal or business decisions (which was almost daily), I often asked myself the simple question, *What's the right thing to do?* Admittedly, everyone's concept of right and wrong is a function of his or her own moral or religious upbringing, but it's a question all of us should ask within the context of our historical character development. In my case, that development was influenced and shaped very dramatically by one very loving and caring woman. Rose Sievert, my mom.

At the age of eighty-three, she took her last breath as she peacefully slept. That was in April of 2001. I miss her loving arms and those nurturing kitchen-table talks.

··············· *For Reflection* ···············
She speaks with wisdom, and faithful instruction is on her tongue. She watches over the affairs of her household and does not eat the bread of idleness. Her children arise and call her blessed; her husband also, and he praises her . . .

Proverbs 31:26–28

··

I am indeed very blessed by a mother who provided so much nurturing. Even years after her death, it astounds me how many of her expressions of love and encouragement regularly come to mind. There isn't a day that goes by in which I am not reminded of things she said during those kitchen-table talks. I could not describe my mother any better than this depiction in Proverbs of a strong woman who not only avoids idleness but provides faithful instruction, watches over the affairs of the household, and is considered blessed by her spouse and children.

Do you have similar memories of your mother's influence on you during your formative years? Think back on what has stayed with you and emerged in your thoughts in recent years. And if those experiences and her words have been submerged in your memory banks and don't often rise to the level of conscious awareness, then perhaps a focused effort to recall them will bring them to the surface.

The responsibilities and the blessings of motherhood are enormous, and not every child's story is as joyful as mine. If you experienced a less than ideal childhood at the hands of an abusive or neglectful mother, and have been blessed with children of your own, you may be seeking to turn that experience into a triumph in your own parenting. Although we can't alter our past experiences, with God's help, we can learn from them and enrich our futures and the futures of our children.

If you are fortunate enough to have a mother who is still living, I encourage you to reach out to her and express your love and gratitude to her often. And if you have children of your own, I encourage you to give them the gift of loving training and nurturing. In that way, such responsible, persistent, and thoughtful parenting can positively impact future generations.

The Accidental Legacy

In the mid-1980s, after several years of working very long hours and regretfully neglecting my family, I became the senior vice-president and CFO of Maccabees Mutual Life Insurance Company in Southfield, Michigan. My career aspirations were coming to fruition but other dimensions of my life were suffering. My three children were young and needed a father, and I knew that my wife, Sue, was carrying almost all of the parenting burden.

Since my actuarial training was a way to leverage my success to a broader network of industry contacts, I'd begun volunteering on a variety of industry and professional boards and committees. I served as an officer and ultimately as president of the Michigan Actuarial Society; I also eagerly agreed to serve on a number of committees and task forces of the American Council of Life Insurance (ACLI), a trade association representing hundreds of insurance companies nationwide. Involvement with the ACLI enabled me to network with some of the top professionals in the insurance industry. While those contacts proved to be valuable, this level of industry service only exacerbated my work/life imbalance. I was away from the family even more and even more guilty.

ACLI committee meetings were almost always held at its corporate offices in Washington, D.C. Typically, I flew from Detroit to Washington the evening before an event, attended the meetings the next day, and returned to Detroit that evening . . . until one Thursday in May 1984 when this pattern finally changed for good.

It started ordinarily enough: Late Thursday I flew into Washington for a Friday meeting of the Actuarial Committee. I checked into my hotel near the Capitol, where someone recommended that I have dinner at "The 1789," a historic restaurant in nearby Georgetown. After packing the documents I needed to read for Friday's meeting, I caught a cab to Georgetown; I was multitasking long before the word found its way into the popular lexicon.

As usual, I watched the city go by through the windows of the cab, pondering tomorrow's meeting. It was a rainy, somewhat cold evening, but the restaurant was quaint and warm. The meal was wonderful and the ambience was rustic but elegant. Since the dining room was too dark to read the documents I had brought along, I found myself intermittently deep in thought or observing others—in despair over my lack of productivity.

A few tables away was Bob Johannsen, a member of the Actuarial Committee who would be attending the meeting with me the next morning. He was eating with a girl of about thirteen or fourteen. As I waited for my dessert to arrive, I began to worry about all the work I wasn't doing, but realizing the futility of this, I decided to shake it off and simply go say hello to Bob.

"Hi, Fred! So good to see you," said Bob warmly. "I'd like you to meet my daughter." Bob explained that he made a practice of bringing his children with him on business trips. "We stay an extra day or two to do some sightseeing."

I listened intently. They both looked so happy. What an excellent way for a busy executive to spend some quality time with his children. My daughters were nine-year-old Heidi, five-year-old Dena, and three-year-old Denise. Bob was just as busy as I was, but here he'd found a way to add at least one element of balance to his life.

When I returned to the hotel, I immediately called Sue and told her about Bob and his daughter. "What would you think of sending Heidi to Washington tomorrow? She and I could do some sightseeing over the weekend."

"That's a terrific idea!" said Sue. And she made the flight arrangements while I arranged for two more nights at the hotel.

I could hardly wait. After Friday's committee meeting, I rushed to the airport. At the age of nine, Heidi was understandably apprehensive about traveling alone for the first time, and I could see the nervousness on her face when she walked off the plane with her airline escort. But once she caught a glimpse of me, she broke into a broad smile. Not only was she relieved but she was finally going to have some time alone with her dad.

I had been to Washington several times, but this was Heidi's first time. We planned two days of visiting major tourist sites: the Vietnam

Memorial, the Washington Monument, the Lincoln Memorial, Arlington National Cemetery, and Ford's Theater where Lincoln was assassinated. The weather was quite nice, so we did a lot of walking, and when we got to the Lincoln Memorial, Heidi begged me to race her up the steps.

"Here's an idea," I said, smiling. "How about if I stand here at the base and time you running up and down?"

Heidi thought this was a great challenge, and when she returned and I told her how long it had taken, she insisted—positively humming with unbounded youthful energy—on running it again in an attempt to beat her previous time. What fun!

At the Vietnam Memorial, I searched the Wall for the name of my junior high and high school friend Arnie Sarna, who had been killed in the war. When I'd heard about the Vietnam Memorial, I was not particularly impressed with the design. But searching for Arnie's name and seeing hundreds of linear feet of personal notes, flowers, and memorabilia placed at the base of the Wall was something else—I couldn't move.

"Why are you crying, Daddy?" Heidi asked, turning to see what I was doing.

I struggled to explain the war and the loss of my friend to her, and suddenly I realized how moved Heidi was. This was important. This was very good—for my daughter to share something so profound, for her to witness me reflecting on something so true and deep.

Here is another deep truth: When I'd boarded the plane for Washington the previous Thursday, I never could have imagined that a seemingly coincidental encounter with Bob Johannsen and his daughter would initiate a practice that would endure for the next twenty-five years—resulting in at least a hundred trips, impacting hundreds more people than my family (but I'll get to that in a minute).

Starting with that first trip with Heidi in 1984, I began taking each of my five children on annual trips alone with me for that special one-on-one bonding time. When the kids were young, a trip up the road to a local hotel for two or three nights was an exciting adventure. As they became teenagers and young adults, we sought out more educational and cultural experiences; the trips got more exotic and often included travel across the country or even overseas. But in each case, the important thing was not where we traveled, but rather the fact that we did it together.

And this trip-taking practice birthed yet another practice: I would eventually talk about this practice of taking trips with my children hundreds of times to thousands of New York Life employees and agents throughout my career—inspiring hundreds of those employees and agents to adopt the same practice with their own children.

Seeing how this single event impacted my career, my family, and my personal happiness, I now realize that God arranged that providential meeting at "The 1789." I also recognize that God knew how the effects of it would ultimately play out over the ensuing years—multiplying the benefits exponentially as I shared our experiences. Even today, years after my retirement, the most frequent comment I receive in emails and holiday greeting cards from members of my extended family at New York Life is a thank-you for sharing the stories of those trips because so many of them adopted a similar practice with their own families.

During eight of the last eleven years of my career, New York Life achieved the number-one market share position in the sale of life insurance in the United States. We achieved many other distinctions and number-one rankings during those years, but I truly believe my greatest legacy to the company was more about my faith and my family values— values that inspired others—than any of those corporate achievements.

·············· *For Reflection* ··············
He will turn the hearts of the parents to their children, and
the hearts of the children to their parents . . .

Malachi 4:6

··

Triggered by a providential meeting in a Georgetown restaurant in 1984, I started a family tradition that would positively impact my life, my family's life, my career, and the lives of hundreds of others. Only God could have arranged that fortuitous meeting, and only God could have known that it would lead to the bonding of hundreds of parents with their children. And only with God's help did I recognize that my real legacy at New York Life Insurance Company was not its financial success and global prominence but rather the family values I shared with the New York Life agents and employees.

Are you struggling as I did with balancing your career aspirations with your spiritual life and your responsibilities as a spouse and parent? Have you developed coping techniques that will allow you to spend more time with your family? If you have developed such techniques, have you shared your family traditions and practices with your friends and colleagues in the hope that they may benefit by adopting similar traditions? I am sure Bob Johannsen did not consciously convey to me his practice of traveling with his daughter in order to influence me or anyone else. But by sharing his practice with me, he positively influenced my life and, indirectly, the lives of thousands of others through my storytelling.

The disease of workaholism and the drive for success by worldly standards is a temptation that can overcome you, as it overcame me. Don't let your ambitions for career success drive a wedge between you and your family. The book of Malachi is concerned with the coming of the Day of the Lord, and God's judgment on the people. Thus, the prophet's words about parents and children are able to express the danger of neglecting the bond between parent and child, and also share the hope that the prophet's words, although they come from a human messenger, will yet have the power to bring the hearts of parents and their children together, and make room for God's mercy.

Like the parents in this passage, I too received a life-changing message from a human source; by God's hand, Bob Johannsen became a divine messenger to me in that providential meeting in the Georgetown restaurant.

Cultural Differences

When my daughter Heidi was twelve and Dena was nine, I took them on a wonderful ten-day trip to Germany and Austria. Only three years had elapsed since I had started the practice of taking each of my children on an annual trip alone with me. With each trip, I realized what a wonderful way it was for a busy, overworked executive like me to find added time to bond with his children.

Most of our trips had an educational element, as we often visited cities with rich histories or national parks with interesting geological significance. To optimize the experience for each child, I usually took just one with me on each of these trips—but since Europe represented a longer trip, I thought it appropriate for the three of us to team up. The girls were excited and liked the idea of being together with Dad.

On the long flight to Europe, I announced their assignment.

"Assignment?" said Heidi.

"Yes," I answered. "The theme of this trip is 'Cultural Differences.' I want you both to be very observant each day of the differences in how Europeans live from how we live in the United States, because every night before we go to bed I'm going to ask you to record your observations in a journal."

As I'd thought, the girls took to their assignment with enthusiasm, making note of a wide range of differences that included, among many others, the extent to which Europeans smoked cigarettes, the fact that we often saw dogs sitting at their masters' tables in restaurants, and that merchants never put change in the customer's hand but rather set it on the counter. There was also one particularly glaring difference: the nudity that was evident in advertising, on public beaches, and at hotel swimming pools.

Early one morning, we were driving from Munich, Germany, to Salzburg, Austria, and the girls had been incessantly begging to go swimming when we arrived in Salzburg. With visions of visiting historic churches, wandering through world-class art museums, and attending concerts and operas in Salzburg, I snapped, "Girls! There are thousands of years of history out there, and I don't want to waste my time sitting next to a swimming pool!"

But their fervent pressure continued and eventually I succumbed. Shortly after we got to our hotel, the girls changed into their cute little swimsuits, I grabbed a book, and we headed for the indoor pool. What we saw next was certainly not what I had planned.

At the entrance to the pool area, we had to climb three or four stairs. As the girls walked single-file up those stairs, what should they see coming down but two young men in their early twenties, totally naked! I was somewhat shocked and realized this may have been the first time my young daughters had seen a naked man up close. Talk about a stark and rapid immersion into cultural differences!

Judging by their body language and facial expressions, the girls were indeed shocked, but they didn't say anything. They simply jumped into the pool and started to play. I was relieved to see the young men depart the pool area, leaving the three of us alone, but my peace did not last long.

Within minutes after I sat down to read my book, the sauna door next to me burst open and out ran three lovely young women in their early twenties, also totally naked. This was the first time I had seen female nudity in public and I was naturally intrigued. You might say it gave me an entirely new perspective on sitting poolside and my own new sense of appreciation for these rapidly accumulating cultural differences. Suddenly I too was participating in the educational exercise.

Unashamedly the naked girls scampered up to the pool and jumped in. This proved too much for Heidi and Dena. Unlike the experience with the men, who had promptly walked away, here my girls were confronting prolonged nudity at close range—as if three strangers were suddenly bathing with them in a relatively small pool. They ran over to me and said, "Daddy, let's get out of here!"

I paused, wondering how I could tease my daughters without appearing too eager to observe their bathing partners. "Hold on just a minute!" I said calmly. "I thought you wanted to swim, and besides, my book is just starting to get interesting!"

Heidi caught my teasing and cleverly responded, "But, Dad, there's thousands of years of history out there!"

The trip turned out to be magnificent. As originally planned, we did enjoy the art, music, and history of the region, and I was less resistant to swimming respites for the remainder of the trip. And yes, we did see more nudity.

Among family and friends, the story of this trip was told often, generating great interest and amusement, but I never considered it legendary . . . until a few years later when my youngest son, Corey, was ten. I had intended to take him on a fishing trip to Alaska. But I was in the middle of a major business deal, and just days before we were to leave, I was forced to cancel.

Expecting Corey to be very disappointed, I broke the bad news to him as I tucked him into bed that evening. "But later this summer," I consoled him, "when this deal is finished, I promise I'll take you to Europe."

I was talking softly. Corey was deep under his blankets and nearly asleep, so I was shocked by what came next. With an explosion of energy, he flung off the covers, leapt out of bed, and, clenching his fists, he yelled, "YES!"

"Corey," I said, startled, "I thought you'd be disappointed."

He looked up at me, excitement in his eyes, and asked, "Dad, when we go there, can we go *swimming*?"

Even as a ten-year-old, he was clearly thinking about the opportunity to see for himself what the girls and I had seen poolside.

Although I was gratified that my youngest son had actually remembered something about the educational objectives of these trips, I realized that before the next trip I'd need to spend a little time educating him on a somewhat broader understanding of the term *cultural differences.*

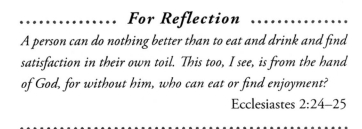

A person can do nothing better than to eat and drink and find satisfaction in their own toil. This too, I see, is from the hand of God, for without him, who can eat or find enjoyment?

Ecclesiastes 2:24–25

The one-on-one annual trips I took with my children over twenty-five years were marvelous bonding experiences for us and also represented a legacy to the employees and agents of New York Life. That legacy probably never would have materialized had I not told hundreds of agents and employees the amusing story of the European trip I took with Dena and Heidi and the sequel involving Corey. Similar stories later became a regular part of my numerous presentations to employees and agents each year.

This particular story did not relate to an embedded message from God but it did set the stage for future storytelling that often disclosed my faith in God and the guidance and nurturing He provided to me in many aspects of my personal, spiritual, and vocational life.

Think back on the memorable experiences you've had with your spouse and children. Is there an amusing story to be told that reflects the love and unity in your family? Cherish those memories, and don't hesitate to share them with your friends and acquaintances. They may more readily recall their own joyful family experiences as a result of hearing yours. As Ecclesiastes 2:24–25 reminds us, we can find fun and enjoyment in our toils—something in which we should rejoice.

Johnny's Yard

Even before we realized we could not conceive, Sue and I had decided we would eventually adopt children; we wanted to extend our love to children most in need of such love and nurturing.

In 1975, we adopted nine-month-old Heidi, who had been abandoned at birth in a basket on the steps of a local church in Seoul, Korea. Following the finalization of Heidi's adoption and her naturalization as a U.S. citizen, we adopted five-month-old Dena in 1979. Dena had been given up for adoption by a twenty-six-year-old unwed mother who left her small village outside of Seoul to secretly deliver her baby.

Since foreign adoptions were complicated and costly, for our third child, we decided to try to adopt locally in Michigan. We submitted all of the paperwork and were very early in the process when we received a call asking us to consider taking a special-needs child out of her existing foster home. Within a day or two we visited Denise—who was then two and a half—and concluded that we would adopt her with full understanding of her special condition.

Denise was not severely disabled, but she had been labeled a "failure-to-thrive infant." Because her birth mother had not properly fed her during her first eighteen months of life, Denise had remained at her birth weight for most of that period—a time during which the brain normally doubles in size. Denise had a number of related issues, including eating disorders, speech problems, and a mental maturity level below her chronological age. She had trouble articulating her thoughts and spoke way too rapidly for most people to understand. She ate voraciously and got quite heavy even at a young age. She also had great difficulty adapting to any kind of change from her daily routine. We were told that it was highly likely that many of these issues would affect her throughout her adult life. But little could any of us have known how Denise would thrive.

The most challenging issue to deal with during Denise's childhood was her education. She attended very good elementary and middle schools in the public school system, but it was always extremely difficult to find classes that both met her needs and gave her room for further development. When placed in special-education classes, she was inadequately challenged and at times mimicked the inappropriate behaviors of her less capable classmates. On the other hand, she simply could not keep pace with the more advanced abilities of non-disabled students in mainstream classes.

In middle school, this dilemma became more pronounced, and after speaking to school officials and psychologists, it became clear that an optimal solution would be to find a private boarding school that might better meet Denise's needs. Sue and I really didn't like the idea of sending Denise away, especially considering her difficulty in adapting to change. And like many parents of special-needs children, we felt guilty—almost as if we were copping out. Nonetheless, after much prayer and consideration, we concluded that a suitable private school would be in her best interest.

On a New York Life business trip, one of my colleagues, Pat Colloton, told Sue and me about Riverview, a unique and well-known school to which he and his wife Patti had sent their son, Johnny. Located in Sandwich, Massachusetts, it was run by a well-known and well-published educator and author, Rick Lavoie, and his wife, Janet. We knew this fortuitous discussion was prompted by God. In the course of our discussions with the Collotons, we also learned of Johnny's tragic drowning death at their home in Kansas City, Missouri. I was surprised I had not heard of this earlier because I had known Pat for a few years and he had never mentioned it. However, I quickly came to understand and appreciate the extent of the devastation to Pat and his family at the loss of their beloved son. Johnny loved his years at Riverview and the Collotons had donated funds in memory of him to establish a small park on the Riverview campus, complete with a gazebo: it was named "Johnny's Yard."

After researching a number of potential schools, we were most impressed with what we learned about Riverview and the Lavoies and we arranged for a visit with Denise during the summer following her sixteenth birthday. We worried she wouldn't like the school or would be extremely nervous about the possibility of leaving home—boy were we surprised!

The visit to Riverview was wonderful! Denise was treated very respectfully and compassionately in her interview with Janet Lavoie. She then visited several summer classes in progress and was warmly welcomed by the teachers and students in each class. As we left the campus, a couple of students thanked her for coming and even yelled out good wishes as we got in the car for the ride home.

During the visit, Denise had been difficult to read, so I had no idea what to expect when I finally asked, "Denise, how do you like the school?"

Without hesitation, she responded, "I want to go there."

Sue and I were amazed! How thrilling that she would respond in this way. Her words were a gift from God, a gift that began during our conversation with Pat Colloton.

That fall, Denise enrolled at Riverview; it was very difficult for Sue and me to drop her off in September, but we knew it was best for her. In subsequent years, the decision repeatedly proved to be a very wise one, as Denise thrived in the Riverview environment. There was probably no place quite like Riverview and surely no place as perfect in meeting Denise's needs. During her years there, Sue and I came to learn that their very simple tag line, "Riverview Cares," appropriately and succinctly describes exactly what Riverview does and what it stands for.

From there, Denise went on to attend Cape Cod Community College. She has remained on the Cape into early adulthood in a very supportive community called Living Independently Forever (LIFE).

At age thirty-two, Denise now has her own condominium in the LIFE community, is a landlord (as she has a tenant living with her), is working part-time during the week, and has many close friends. Riverview changed her life, enabled her to join LIFE, and indeed prepared her to live independently forever.

How did she get to this point? There were many highlights and emotional experiences related to Denise's years at Riverview, but none were more memorable than her graduation ceremony. For Riverview students, this was perhaps the biggest day of their lives.

It was celebrated in an auditorium at Cape Cod Community College. Despite a relatively small graduating class, the audience that summer day in 1999 numbered several hundred, with all of the faculty, staff, and numerous family members and friends in attendance. Our entire family came, and I sat in the center of a row occupied almost exclusively by Sieverts. The ceremony not only recognized all of the graduating seniors and involved presentations and speeches by some of the students, but it also included a handful of special awards.

We burst with pride as Denise walked up to receive her diploma with a broad smile amid the cheers of her classmates. Up and down our row, the Sieverts were unanimously fighting back tears, and I couldn't help but surmise that in most public schools, a ceremony like this would have been for Denise a welcomed ending to a less-than-satisfying experience. At Riverview, however, it was a triumph—a true "commencement" of a meaningful and fulfilling life for the students and their families and a well-deserved recognition of the faculty and administration for a job well done.

Following the graduation ceremony, Rick Lavoie got up to introduce the winners of a few special awards. When he got to the good citizenship award, he explained that it had been established in memory of Johnny Colloton and was being presented to the student who best exemplified Johnny's spirit of friendship and caring for his fellow classmates.

He then paused and said, "Fred Sievert is in the audience today."

I was surprised and all my family members stared at me with equal surprise.

"Fred is a friend and colleague of Johnny's father, Pat Colloton," continued Rick. "And on almost every visit to campus, Fred sits in Johnny's Yard and calls his friend Pat to tell him how well maintained the yard is and how beautiful it looks. Pat has always greatly appreciated those calls."

Rick was right. Out of gratitude to Pat for introducing us to Riverview, I had done exactly what he described—but to my knowledge, Pat was the only one who knew about those calls.

"Today is a special day," continued Rick. "For today, Fred can leave this ceremony, go to Johnny's Yard, call his friend Pat, and tell Pat that his daughter Denise has been awarded the Johnny Colloton Good Citizenship Award."

What a dramatic and moving way to make the award to Denise! I could barely focus through my tears as Denise marched up to the stage—to the enthusiastic applause of all her classmates and their families. My family was as stunned as I was. It was clearly a fitting recognition of our daughter, who had become a kind, loving, and fully-accepted "special" person in this Riverview community.

That afternoon I went alone to Johnny's Yard and called Pat. We both cried so hard as I told him the whole story that I was barely able to articulate the words. I will be eternally grateful for the partnership of God and Pat Colloton and the resulting opportunity that came to Denise—one that changed her life forever.

·············· *For Reflection* ··············
*Who shall separate us from the love of Christ? Shall trouble
or hardship or persecution or famine or nakedness or danger
or sword? As it is written: "For your sake we face death all
day long; we are considered as sheep to be slaughtered." No,
in all these things we are more than conquerors through him
who loved us.*

Romans 8:35–37

As Sue and I reluctantly tried to find a residential school that would meet the requirements of our special-needs daughter, Denise, we were led to Riverview School in Massachusetts by God and by my colleague, Pat Colloton. In a sense, through God's grace, Johnny's death provided a means by which the Collotons would find a triumphant way to touch other lives and impact Sue, me, and Denise in a very meaningful way.

Denise feared and poorly handled change of any sort. Miraculously, Riverview proved to be the perfect place where she could not only overcome her fears but where she would develop and flourish—something we didn't fully appreciate until that highly emotional experience on the day of her graduation. It was a bonus when that emotional experience involved Pat Colloton and his deceased son, Johnny. God's hand was most certainly in the events at Riverview from matriculation to graduation. The tragic death of Johnny Colloton ultimately resulted in emotional healing and triumphs for both the Collotons and the Sieverts.

If you or your children are plagued with fears, hardships, or anxieties, remember Paul's words to the Romans through which he is seeking to alleviate the fear of separation from God's love and care: No hardship, trouble, or persecution can separate us from the love of Christ. We are more than conquerors through Him who loved us.

Denise's Riverview experience is a story of triumph over adversity for someone who deeply believes in and embraces the love of Christ. And the Collotons found a degree of peace and comfort in extending their love and Johnny's love through this providential experience.

Discovery in Korea

When we adopted our daughter Dena, a Korean orphan, at the age of five months in early 1979, we knew only a few basics about her background—that she was given up for adoption by her unwed mother and was living with a foster mother until she could make the long flight to the United States to join our family.

We actually started the adoption process with the Dillon Adoption Agency years before Dena was even born, but unlike the relatively straightforward adoption of her older sister, Heidi, the bureaucratic delays seemed to drag on forever. But our adoption proved to be well worth the wait; Dena has been a wonderful, loving, and happy person who has blessed our family dearly.

Dena's strong faith and compassion have also blessed the lives of others. During her teen years, she often provided comfort to the sick and elderly. Before going away to college, she often spent time simply sitting and talking to some of the elderly residents at the Waveny Nursing Home in New Canaan, Connecticut. One elderly blind lady there was as sad as we were when Dena went off to Calvin College in Michigan for her undergraduate studies.

As a college student, Dena arranged to spend a semester abroad in China during the fall of 1999. Before her departure, I asked if for our annual trip I could meet her in Korea on her way back from China in December. She was excited by the prospect and I began to plan the trip.

Although Dena had never asked much about her birth parents or the circumstances surrounding her adoption, I thought it appropriate to offer to do everything possible to discover more. That summer, as we were planning for Korea, I asked Dena if she wanted me to try to track down information about her birth parents.

"No, Dad," she quickly responded, "you and Mom are my parents."

Sue and I were deeply moved, but, even so, we wished we could do something to fill in Dena's knowledge of her ancestry.

Nevertheless, I didn't think about the matter again. That December, we met in Seoul and had a wonderful three days together despite the cold weather and the difficulty of finding anyone who spoke English. In fact, during the entire trip we encountered very few Caucasians. I stood out quite noticeably as a tall American Caucasian man, but many people approached Dena expecting her to be fluent in Korean. She actually felt quite at home!

After observing Dena's wonder at visiting this beautiful country of her ancestry, I asked if she'd like to visit one of the many orphanages in Seoul so she could see what life might have been like for her if she hadn't been adopted. Although I'm not sure she eagerly embraced the idea, she agreed.

The next morning, when we arrived at the local orphanage, we were greeted warmly by its executive director. He took us on a tour, and Dena got to play with many of the preschoolers while the older students were in school. It seemed clean and well run, but it was clearly missing the most important element of an ideal home: loving and nurturing parents. Even though she seemed to be enjoying the visit, I realized that Dena's mind must be wandering into "what-if" territory.

The executive director told us that twenty years earlier, when we adopted Dena, he was the executive director of a nearby adoption agency and he suggested that we visit—to see what it would have been like for Dena to visit such an agency for periodic medical visits. He wrote down the address and our driver took us.

The place was bustling with foster mothers and infants, and realizing that she was once such a babe in the arms of her foster mother must have given Dena an unusual emotional sensation. *How wonderful*, I thought, *that those women volunteered in such a way with babies who were largely rejected by their society. Thank God for these heroines and for the care such women had given our beloved Dena.*

Before we left, our young guide had one question. "Do you remember Dena's Korean name?" she asked me.

"Jung Ja Moon," I responded and I gave her Dena's birth date.

To our delight and surprise, Dena was in the agency's database, but the only information was the name of the adoption agency.

"Why don't you visit the Dillon Adoption Agency?" our guide suggested. "It's only a few miles up the road."

In a definite change from her reticent attitude in August, Dena was eager to go. Both of us had begun to sense that this was destined to be—that God was guiding us on this journey.

At the Dillon Adoption Agency, we were once again greeted by a young woman who also found Dena on her agency's database. "Please wait here," she told us, leaving us in her small, cluttered office. Then three or four minutes later she returned with a three-inch-thick file.

We had been told almost nothing when we adopted Dena in 1979, but now we were amazed to witness the Koreans' extensive recordkeeping.

"Shall we look?" asked the guide.

"Yes, please," we answered. And embedded in the file we found the original handwritten application documents Sue and I had filled out—filling my heart with a present-day reprise of the excitement and anticipation Sue and I had felt at the possibility of adding another daughter to our young family twenty years ago.

For more than an hour, Dena and I listened intently as this young and dedicated agency representative translated the file contents. She read transcripts of interviews with Dena's birth mother that supplied the details of the family and personal situation that led to her baby being placed for adoption. She was unwed and age twenty-six and was no longer dating the baby's biological father. The disgrace of having a baby out of wedlock was not easily tolerated in her culture, and it was compounded by an additional level of disgrace for placing a baby up for adoption. The solution to dealing with both of these issues was for Dena's mother to leave home temporarily while she delivered the baby and arranged for an adoption. We were enthralled by this story, and particularly moved by the photographs of Dena and her foster mother.

Even if I had spent months on the phone or writing letters, I could not have located this information. Our success depended on personal visits to the right locations—visits that could only have been guided by the loving hands of God. This was much more than a coincidence.

We left with a copy of the file but without making an attempt to locate Dena's birth mother. Considering the secret circumstances of her daughter's birth, we felt it would have been inappropriate to track her down and possibly embarrass her in front of her current family.

Nevertheless, we came home with deep satisfaction, gratitude to God, and a sense of closure. We now knew the circumstances surrounding Dena's adoption and were grateful that her birth mother had decided to offer up precious little Jung Ja Moon.

As it turned out, God wasn't yet finished with this experience.

More than a decade after our trip to Korea, Dena and her husband, Doug, arranged through an adoption agency to travel to Korea in 2010 to make contact with Dena's birth mother. Although she was initially reluctant to meet, Dena's birth mother agreed on the condition that it would be a secret and private meeting. We had been right: her current family members were unaware of the birth, and such a revelation would have been shameful and embarrassing for her mother.

The meeting did take place; in fact, the three of them met three separate times during the trip and agreed to maintain contact through the adoption agency. Doug and Dena both described it as the experience of a lifetime. I can only believe that God facilitated this reunion on a timetable and in a way that overcame the very real cultural obstacles that would have normally prevented such an emotionally satisfying meeting for all of them.

·············· *For Reflection* ···············

He called a little child to him, and placed the child among them. And he said: "Truly I tell you, unless you change and become like little children, you will never enter the kingdom of heaven. Therefore, whoever takes the lowly position of this child is the greatest in the kingdom of heaven. And whoever welcomes one such child in my name welcomes me."

Matthew 18:2–5

My annual trips with each of my five children were marvelous bonding experiences and created wonderful memories that the children will certainly remember long after I am gone. Even as they became adults we continued to look for opportunities for such travel. The trip to Korea with Dena became far more than a simple bonding experience. With God's guiding hand, we learned a great deal about her family origins, knowledge that ultimately led to a wonderful unanticipated reunion with her biological mother.

What we have learned through our experience of adoption is that we are all God's children and that biological origins really don't matter at all. We love our adopted daughters as much as our natural-born sons. They are all miraculous gifts from God to us, and we take our parenting responsibility very seriously. This was reinforced through the providential discovery of Dena's biological mother and Dena's ultimate meeting with her. We welcomed Dena into our home in the name of Christ, and Matthew 18:5 took on new meaning as we recognized that welcoming her was in effect welcoming the Lord.

Regardless of whether you have adopted a child, can you consider that your children are gifts from God and need to be welcomed in His name? Be assured, they look to you as role models, whether you realize it or not. If they are adopted, can you see how, like Dena, they view you as their mother and father regardless of whether those ties are biological? As Jesus tells us in Matthew 18:3, we can benefit and learn from their unconditional love and unfailing faith. Jesus tells us as adults that "unless you change and become like little children, you will never enter the kingdom of heaven."

Finding Roots in Poland

I had traveled much of the world, but I'd never explored my roots; the task seemed so overwhelmingly difficult that I never gave it a second thought. But in May 2009 when Sue and I decided to take a two-week tour of Eastern Europe, I was excited. We would focus on Poland, the original home of my maternal grandfather, Ignatius Matusiak. The appeal of Poland was fourfold: (1) we had never been there; (2) it was part of my ancestral background; (3) I had always wanted to visit Auschwitz; and (4) the trip was highly recommended by some dear friends who had visited the country several times.

Before this trip, the only things I'd known about my grandfather were what my mother had told me: his name, that he came to America on "the boat," and that he lied about his age—saying he was eighteen when he was really fifteen—to avoid being denied access to a ship. Those scanty facts certainly didn't seem like enough information to begin a genealogical search.

The plan was to spend three nights in Krakow before going on to Warsaw. While in Krakow, we spent a day on a private tour of the Auschwitz-Birkenau death camps, which was far more intense than I had anticipated. For the first time in my life I sobbed uncontrollably. Perhaps it was my Christian faith or my German heritage (on my father's side). Perhaps it was the exhibit of human hair, four or five feet deep in a room that was sixty feet long and fifteen feet wide. We were told this much hair was clipped from the bodies before cremation . . . every single day! Perhaps it was the whole thing.

I was speechless as I observed the Auschwitz exhibits and the gas chambers and crematoria of Birkenau, where every day 10,000 human beings were exterminated and cremated. If ever anything could test my faith, it's wondering how and why God didn't intervene more quickly to stop this. My faith has not faltered but I have some tough questions to ask when I get to the other side.

The next day, our third afternoon in Krakow, we decided to look up my mother's maiden name in the local telephone book. The thought of my ancestors living in Poland but leaving before the Nazi era somehow inspired me to see what we could find. *What if my grandfather had not left in 1909?* I wondered. *Would he have known what the Nazis were doing in his country? Would he have been killed in the war? Would he have been part of the resistance movement?*

It took us a few hours to locate a phone book; we started at the hotel's front desk, went to the local post office, and were finally directed to a cellular telephone shop in a downtown shopping mall. There was one Matusiak in the Krakow phone book with an address for a shop in the town square that was literally less than a hundred yards from our hotel. Sue and I thought the same thing: *God is putting us in touch with my grandfather's Polish relatives!*

Hurriedly we made our way to the Matusiak craft and jewelry shop only to learn that the employees did not speak English—but, thanks to a customer who served as an interpreter, we learned that Mr. and Mrs. Matusiak were out of town. We left handwritten notes for them with contact information but never heard back. We struck out!

However, given the unlikely possibility that we would return any time soon, I was unwilling to give up—I had an idea.

As we packed our bags to leave Krakow that afternoon, I emailed my assistant in Connecticut and asked her to search Michigan's Wayne County death records—I thought I remembered my grandfather dying in Detroit when I was in high school. She found his death record easily, which indicated a birth date of July 25, 1894.

"Can you search the Ellis Island database for an Ignatius Matusiak?" I typed by return email. "Look for someone who might have arrived in New York sometime between 1905 and 1915."

To our delight, she found just one Ignatius Matusiak who'd arrived in 1909 and gave his age as eighteen, which was precisely consistent with my mother's account. According to the death record, he was born in 1894 and would have been fifteen in 1909.

The Ellis Island entry card indicated he was Austrian Polish, and his last place of residence was a town called Bulowice. Imagine our excitement: within just a few hours of that first email to my assistant, we had found him—not to mention his birth date, his hometown, and his arrival date at Ellis Island.

When we learned that Bulowice was only thirty miles away, we asked the hotel if we could keep our room for one more night. Fortunately for us, there was one room available in the hotel that night. Surely God's hand was in this. We went to bed not knowing what to expect, but we were thrilled by the potential adventure ahead.

The next morning our English-speaking driver took us an hour away to the quaint town of Bulowice, nestled in the rolling hills of western Poland—less than five miles from Auschwitz! Again I thought of what might have happened if my grandfather had not emigrated in 1909. *Would he have remained in this town where the smell of burning flesh wafted daily? Would he have known what that smell was? Would he have discovered the truth of the Nazi co-option of his homeland for the systematic, state-sponsored murder of millions? And how would he have confronted the extremely difficult ethical decision either to remain silent and complicit or to become part of the resistance movement?* It is frightening to think of how this may have affected his life and perhaps ultimately my own.

The driver had never before been to Bulowice but he eagerly told us he had been on many such genealogical searches. He knew from experience to take us to the only Catholic church in town, and when we arrived he rang the bell at the parsonage. Though the conversation through the intercom took place entirely in Polish, it was clear that the priest was uninterested in helping us. But our driver was persistent and the priest finally let us in.

As our driver interpreted, the priest listened to our story with a face blank of expression. Then he pulled a large book off the shelf behind his desk—birth records, 1873 through 1898. Repeatedly he searched through the entries for July 1894 but there was no Ignatius Matusiak. We were about to leave when I remembered the issue of my grandfather's age—fifteen versus eighteen. "Would you look up July 1891?" I politely asked him through our driver. And once again the priest scanned the book.

Perhaps my grandfather had simply lived here before he emigrated but had not been born in this town. I was about to accept defeat, when suddenly the priest uttered something in Polish to our driver—and for the first time a smile crossed his face.

There was Grandpa Matusiak, born on July 25, 1891, right in this little village! The priest pointed to the beautiful handwritten calligraphy naming the place and date of his birth, his mother's and father's names, the names of all four of his grandparents, his godparents' names, and even the name of the midwife who delivered Ignatius in his parents' home!

Ecstatic, we recorded all of the information and photographed the appropriate pages of the book. The priest, who had finally warmed up to us, gave us a tour of the church, which had been built in 1817. He claimed that it still looked exactly as it had when my grandfather was baptized at the altar in 1891. In this very place, 118 years earlier, the same God that we worship today had presided over this blessed sacrament— just as He had presided at my mother's baptism, my baptism, and my children's baptisms. I suspected that an omniscient God knew in 1891 that we would be standing in that same spot in 2009.

Sue and I were absolutely delighted and felt certain it was God who had given us this wonderful experience in the middle of an already exciting trip. We were totally satisfied and didn't think about pursuing the matter any further. But little did we know that God and our Polish driver had more in mind for us.

Next, as he had done on many prior searches of this type, the driver took us to the town cemetery, where we found more than twenty tombstones memorializing other Matusiaks. We photographed every Matusiak gravestone; with those birth and death dates in hand, we could easily return to the Bulowice Catholic Church in the future to develop a full family tree.

Again, we were satisfied and prepared to go back to our hotel to finish packing for the trip to Warsaw. But our enthusiastic and aggressive driver had other plans: We were headed to the home of the mayor of Bulowice. We were concerned that the driver might be overstepping his welcome, and we were naturally somewhat reluctant to impose on the mayor. But sensing God's involvement, we went with the flow.

To our amusement, the driver stopped numerous passersby to ask for directions to the mayor's house, and within a few minutes we were ringing his doorbell. He graciously invited us into his home; while the driver related our entire story, the mayor's wife and daughter prepared drinks and snacks for us. They seemed genuinely happy to invite us in and guide us further on our journey of discovery.

The mayor and his family spoke no English, but we sensed what he was doing when he got on his cell phone and began calling current Matusiak residents to explain our story. After several such apparently productive calls, we finished our snack, hugged the mayor's wife and daughter good-bye, and left with the mayor himself. He drove us to the site where my grandfather was born and then to the workplace of the home's current owner to chat with him about what he knew of the former residents.

We learned that the actual house in which my grandfather had been born had burned down in the early 1920s and had later been rebuilt by the current owner's grandfather. The current owner knew little about any earlier residents but seemed very interested in our story. "The elderly woman who lives next door might know more," he told us.

So back to the birth site we went. There, we were able to visit with the neighbor, a woman in her late eighties or early nineties, who was delighted to tell us about members of the Matusiak family that she remembered from "next door." My grandfather left in 1909, so she had not known him personally, but she named numerous other family members who had left for America, many of them destined for Chicago or Detroit.

How strange it must have been for Bulowice residents to see so many friends, family members, and neighbors leave for America—and then never see them again. Perhaps this woman lost a boyfriend or lover to the allure of a life in America, the land of opportunity. As she waved good-bye, we could see in her eyes that she was sad to see us go.

We had learned so much more than we had ever imagined possible. Surely we had gathered every possible bit of information available. But by then we should have known that God held still more in store.

Our final stop on the mayor's guided tour was a visit to the home of the oldest living Matusiak in town. A woman in her eighties, she was a family historian and told story after story of my ancestors who had lived in Bulowice a century earlier. While she was too young to have known Ignatius, she did know his name and knew many relatives whom she suspected were cousins. She too had a likely connection to Ignatius based on his parents' names from the birth records. She showed us the gravestones of her own grandparents, which were prominently displayed in her backyard.

Her husband and her brother lived with her and invited us in for drinks and more food. Our driver, the indefatigable interpreter, translated for us, and they thoroughly enjoyed our meeting and conversation. After a lovely visit, we left with our driver and enthusiastically thanked our hosts and the mayor. As we left, the mayor gave Sue a lapel pin that proudly displayed the name of his town, and then he kissed her hand.

What an exciting twenty-four hours! The providential digression from our planned itinerary resulted in many revelations, some of them quite profound. It turned out that Ignatius hadn't lied about his age on the boat to America; he really *had been* eighteen. He had lied to everyone else, and he maintained that lie throughout his life. Perhaps he subtracted those three years in order to make himself seem younger; he was actually twenty-five when he met my grandmother, who was fifteen at the time. Perhaps he told her the truth. Perhaps she told him it wouldn't work. Perhaps he was so in love with her that he was unwilling to give up and thereafter declared himself three years younger.

One impression from this experience will remain with me forever. In this idyllic western Poland town in 1909—three years before the sinking of the *Titanic*—an intrepid eighteen-year-old boy left his home, his parents, and the rest of his family to travel to America. He and millions of others who viewed the liberty and opportunity in this country worthy of that personal sacrifice simply would not give up.

I thank God that Grandpa left Poland before World War II and never knew the fumes of the ovens of Birkenau or faced the gut-wrenching decision of how to deal with the knowledge of a genocide playing out in his own backyard.

Though he wrote letters and sent money, Grandpa never returned to Poland. My recollection of him, now enriched by this marvelous experience, was that of a happy man very proud of the family he raised here in *his* America.

················· *For Reflection* ···············
My people, hear my teaching; listen to the words of my mouth. I will open my mouth with a parable; I will utter hidden things, things from of old— things we have heard and known, things our ancestors have told us. We will not hide them from their descendants; we will tell the next generation the praiseworthy deeds of the Lord, his power, and the wonders he has done.

Psalm 78:1–4

Few of us take the time to ask our parents and grandparents about the passions and the exploits of their ancestors—and those recollections are then lost forever as death claims our elderly family members. While I missed the opportunity to learn about my ancestors directly from my own family, how blessed I was that on a trip to Poland with my wife, Sue, God revealed to me what my own grandfather sacrificed and left behind in order to pursue his dream.

The fact that he left an idyllic village in close proximity to Auschwitz and Birkenau, death camps that would soon thereafter become the epicenter for evil in the world, makes the story even more intriguing. Only God knows how the lives of my parents and hence my own existence would have developed differently if Ignatius hadn't had the courage and wanderlust to pursue his dreams in America. And what a shame that I never thought to discuss with him his youthful adventures before his death.

If you have living parents or grandparents, you can be certain they have interesting and wonderful stories to tell of their own life journey and encounters with God. Perhaps you will hear echoes of your own characteristics in the stories of their lives. Don't make the mistake I made and miss the opportunity to learn from their experiences and to express your wonder and appreciation for their sacrifices. Chances are good that they too were guided and nurtured by our loving God in a way that has impacted your life in ways of which you may be unaware.

As the Psalmist indicates at the beginning of Psalm 78, it is important to pass from one generation to another the stories of our ancestors' faith traditions as well as their encounters with, and promises from, God.

Creation Versus Evolution

In the 1980s, our young family was living in a suburb of Detroit. Since both Sue and I were raised in Detroit, we knew the area well; as often as possible we took short, local day trips so we could spend time together.

One of our favorite trips was to the Toledo Zoo, about a one-hour drive from our home. A highly rated zoo, it was relatively compact and easy to cover in three or four hours with five young children.

The zoo had been successfully breeding gorillas for zoos around the nation for a number of years. I have always been fascinated by gorillas; I could stand all day watching them play, groom each other, eat, and sleep. What fascinated me most were their human-like qualities and behaviors, and what captivated me most were the spiritual thoughts and questions that inevitably surfaced as I observed them.

For centuries, people have questioned whether God created humans as a distinct and intellectually superior species (as in the biblical story of creation), or if humans evolved from apes over many millennia of successive mutations (as scientists have theorized). I could fully understand how this issue had confounded both theologians and scientists over the centuries, and the controversy surrounding the famous and highly publicized Scopes Trial of 1925 was not surprising to me.

John Scopes was a Tennessee high school teacher accused of violating a state law that prohibited the teaching of any theory that denied the biblical story of divine creation. The trial, which concerned a relatively simple legal question, ultimately became an internationally publicized debate between well-known prosecuting attorney William Jennings Bryant and defense attorney Clarence Darrow, who battled over the inherent conflict between evolutionary theory and the biblical account of divine creation. Most of the evidence and testimony regarding evolution and creation was deemed inadmissible. Scopes was convicted of technically violating state law but was given only a very nominal monetary fine. The widespread public fascination with the trial demonstrates the emotion surrounding the broader theological and scientific questions it raised.

As I stood watching the huge primates interact at the zoo, my struggle with these issues was an internal one, related to the impact such questions had on my own faith. Even as a young adult, I believed in God and very strongly believed that God had created the universe and all of the creatures and life forms inhabiting it. For me, divine creation was never in doubt; rather, I wondered whether God had created gorillas and apes as an independent species from humans—or whether God's original creation had in fact mutated and evolved over time into humans.

Though I tried to be unbiased, I seriously doubted that the first ape evolved without a divine hand in its creation. Given my strong math and science background and my training in probability and statistics during my actuarial education, I simply could not believe that, even over a period of millions of years, an ape or a human could evolve of its own accord from a single-cell amoebic life form. I found it far more credible to believe that only a higher divine power could be responsible for such complex physical creatures. And even if I could convince myself of an evolutionary theory, how was the first amoeba created? To me, God is real and is the originator of life on earth in all its forms.

Nonetheless, the scientific elements of my education make it impossible for me to deny that adaptive mutations do in fact occur. I know some theologians may argue this point, but I don't buy it. Animals and plant life can and do adapt, something that has been proven through much scientific experimentation. Moreover, I believe God bestowed living beings with this adaptability.

In 1989, when my youngest son, Corey, was eighteen months old, we took the family to the Toledo Zoo one Saturday afternoon. In my usual fashion, I made a beeline for the gorilla exhibit, which was viewed through a floor-to-ceiling glass window that provided a look at both the outdoor play area and the large indoor area with trees, ropes to swing from, and various rock ledges. In the indoor exhibit room that day were several adult gorillas, a couple of adolescents, and one toddler who seemed very close to Corey's size and age.

A fairly large crowd of visitors made it somewhat difficult to work our way up to the glass windows. When we finally maneuvered through the crowd to the front, Corey had perhaps the best view. The crowd was loud—animated and laughing—but suddenly all that changed.

As Corey gazed through the window, he pressed both hands flat against the glass. Seeing him, the toddler gorilla jumped onto a two-foot rock ledge against the glass observation window, walked slowly over to where Corey was standing, and assumed exactly the same posture as Corey. His legs were spread at about shoulder width and his hands were opened and pressed against the inside glass, precisely opposite Corey's hands. For a few amazing minutes, they stood quietly admiring each other, probably wishing the glass barrier weren't separating them from playful interaction. The astounded crowd turned eerily silent—many likely marveling over the obvious connection between the species.

To this day that image is etched in my memory—it has caused me to realize that an abandoned human baby would probably be accepted into, and raised by, such a family of gorillas. There was a bridge that day across the species that bonded and united the hearts and minds of those too young to feel threatened by a potentially dangerous playmate. What is it about humans who, in spite of their superior intellect and communication skills, have such a difficult time coexisting on the planet? What is it that causes wars and destruction when the instincts of these young ones are to accept one another as fellow global companions, even across species?

Without the glass barrier, Corey would have been very vulnerable to a mother gorilla, who would have been strong enough to tear him to shreds if she felt threatened by the two toddlers touching. But would the mother gorilla do that? Might she instead peacefully accept such playful interactions between two infants so similar in so many ways? Watching their interaction, I focused on the trust and ease with which the young of the two species approached and observed each other. Surely God had instilled such confidence and trust in both our young and the young of our primate relatives.

I find myself fascinated more by the similarities than the differences in the species for other reasons. The natural bond between animals of any species is a reaffirmation to me of God's love and of the wonder of creation. For me, the complexities of the physical capabilities and features of every species give witness to God's hand in all creation. The natural attraction and bond between an eighteen-month-old human and an eighteen-month-old gorilla tells me we were created to live in peace and harmony as fellow inhabitants of the planet.

Like the arguments in the Scopes Trial, this brief interaction between species could be interpreted in many different ways. Some might suggest it is evidence that humans have indeed evolved from these less sophisticated creatures with their natural familial affinity for one another. Some might think, as I briefly did, of the danger of a powerful mother gorilla protecting her young—and might suggest that survival of the fittest would never have allowed humans to evolve and survive when apes are so much more powerful. Still others might believe that apes would have become extinct due to their intellectual inferiority. And some might point to many failed experiments to artificially inseminate apes using human sperm as evidence that the species indeed are distinct and not genetically compatible.

It may belie my divinity school education, but for me such a debate is not terribly important. I see God's divine hand in creation and I marvel at the bond shared by the natural world and the human inhabitants of earth.

Many years after that incident at the Toledo Zoo, I was given even greater insight into the issues with which I grappled—this time in a rain forest halfway around the world, again involving Corey and a toddler gorilla.

In the summer of 2008, as I was entering my second year as a graduate student at Yale Divinity School, Sue and I traveled with Corey and Zac to Africa. We had planned the trip for more than a year and had carefully chosen sites to visit in Rwanda, Namibia, Botswana, and South Africa. I was most excited about the trip to Rwanda, as we had arranged to trek through the rain forests of the Rwandan mountains to observe families of mountain gorillas in their natural habitat.

After a very long journey, we arrived and spent the evening before our first trek at our lodge at the base of the mountain. I could hardly sleep in anticipation of walking among the gorillas without the protective barrier of a glass wall in a fabricated zoological exhibit.

The next morning we were given a training session by our guides. Then our small group of eight tourists and four guides armed with automatic rifles began ascending the mountain. The rifles were not to be used on the typically gentle and herbivorous gorillas but were for protection against poachers and other insurgent guerillas. Only a few weeks earlier, poachers had massacred an entire family of mountain gorillas in this same vicinity, and the well-publicized story was fresh on the minds of all in our group. During the training, our guides indicated it was illegal to get closer than seven meters to any gorilla—but without a protective glass barrier, that seemed dangerously close to us.

About an hour into our hike, we discovered a family of seventeen gorillas eating the jungle vegetation at the edge of the rain forest. Words can't describe our excitement and awe as we approached these giant but gentle creatures in their natural setting. They slowly and quietly moved along the forest's edge, stopping to eat and occasionally to climb a tree or to groom each other. The adolescents didn't seem as playful in the wild as they were in the zoo; foraging for food was serious business.

A couple of the adult females were carrying and nursing very young infants; there was also a toddler among the pack, whom I judged to be between eighteen and twenty-four months old. For two or three glorious hours, we stood within twenty or thirty feet of this gorilla family, observing and snapping photographs.

Once again, my mind turned to the wonder of creation, this time without much consideration of evolution. There was far too much to observe and think about to waste time contemplating who came first or how the species were similar or different. This was a time to marvel over God's creation and the peacefulness in which God intended us to coexist with these magnificent creatures.

In a wonderful moment of *déjà vu*, the small toddler moved away from the group and began to closely follow Corey. Now twenty years old and over six feet tall, he was the chosen playmate of this young gorilla toddler. The guides kept warning Corey to back up in order to maintain the seven-meter safety cushion, but each time Corey backed up, the toddler followed him. This playful little guy would scamper up to within three or four feet of Corey, and then come to a slow crawl or stop just short of being close enough to touch him.

I couldn't avoid thinking about the zoo and my conjecture that the glass barrier was so important in protecting both the humans and the gorillas. My presumption in Toledo that the mother gorilla might violently defend her young was convincingly proven wrong. The adult gorillas were still very close to us but seemed completely unconcerned that one of their young was approaching a human being.

The initial experience at the zoo had triggered many thoughts about creation and evolution; the experience in Rwanda brought them back. But through these experiences God was telling me that, in time, answers would be revealed to me—but most important was my faith and my renewed celebration in the grandeur of God's creation in *all* its forms.

.... *For Reflection* ....

And God said, "Let the land produce living creatures according to their kinds: the livestock, the creatures that move along the ground, and the wild animals, each according to its kind." And it was so. God made the wild animals according to their kinds, the livestock according to their kinds, and all the creatures that move along the ground according to their kinds. And God saw that it was good.

Genesis 1:24–25

One of the difficult issues I have at times pondered is the role of evolution in animal and human history. I often spend too much time trying to analyze and understand the apparent conflicts between science and religion and not enough time marveling at God's creation. It wasn't until I had these amusing and enlightening experiences with gorillas—both in captivity and in the wild—that I realized that no matter how life forms have changed, mutated, or evolved, God is consistently revealed through the miracle of creation.

The biblical account of creation is a beautiful story that some think is mythical. They point to similar but different creation stories of many other religious traditions as evidence that all religions need to provide some explanation for our origins and that none of the stories can be considered factual. As we look at those stories and their differences, we can't help but wonder if any of them contain elements of truth. In that wonderment it's easy to lose sight of the incredible reality that life in many varied forms actually exists! The marvel to me is not *how* we were created but rather the very fact that we *exist*.

Have there been times in your life when your faith was challenged by apparent conflicts between religious beliefs and the discoveries of science? What are some of the more perplexing questions raised by these conflicts? Can you think of any examples in which God provided at least partial answers, or alternatively assured you that your faith was more important than immediate answers? Maybe it wasn't done literally in a day, and maybe some transitional mutations occurred within and among species, but let's continue to cherish the biblical account in Genesis 1, and let's celebrate and express gratitude to God for the beauty, complexity, and diversity of life that surrounds us daily.

Chapter 6 Exercises

I feel closest to God when I am enjoying time with my family. From the date of our marriage, through the adoptions of our daughters, the births of our sons, and through hundreds, if not thousands, of subsequent blessed events and experiences, my faith journey has taken on new meaning and a greater awareness of God's love. I believe God blesses us richly in the sanctity of marriage and in the relationships within our families. At the same time, He blesses us, God also entrusts us with enormous responsibilities to support our families and to raise, develop, and spiritually nourish our children. Chapter 6 tells numerous stories of my encounters with God in precious familial relationships.

A Mother's Love

As a man, I can imagine but never fully appreciate the bond that usually occurs when a child is conceived in its mother's womb, is carried through many months of pregnancy, and ultimately emerges from the painful but joyous birthing process. There are, of course, examples of mothers who reject, neglect, or abuse their own children, but such children are no less loved by God and often are blessed with a loving home like my own adopted daughter Denise who was neglected as an infant. A good mother's love is from God. In the story "Memories of Mom," I tell just two among many wonderful memories of times when my mother's unconditional love gave me the support, the encouragement, and the moral foundation that have lasted a lifetime.

- What are your fondest memories of your mother that have most positively influenced you since childhood?
- Are you creating similar memories for your children?
- Whatever your gender or age and irrespective of any past mistakes you have made in parenting, what can you do now to nurture your children (even as adults) or to mend the wounds of earlier mistakes? It's never too late to reach out with parental love.

Balancing Your Life

Despite my obsessive type-A personality and workaholic behaviors, I have found some coping techniques that allowed me to capture a modicum of quality time with God and with my family. I've arisen early every morning to work out, to read the Bible, to pray, and to send email messages to my kids and to my wife. But perhaps the most meaningful and important practice was that of taking one-on-one trips with each of my five children annually. As the title of the story indicates, the practice became an "Accidental Legacy" as I retold my experiences to thousands of New York Life agents and employees, many of whom successfully adopted the same practice.

- Do you feel you are adequately balancing your work life with time for your family and your spiritual nourishment?
- If you've enjoyed successes in this regard, will you share your "coping techniques" with your family, friends, and fellow believers?
- If you still sense an imbalance, what concrete steps can you take to begin to rebalance?

Realizing Potential

I get choked up with a painful lump in my throat every time I reread "Johnny's Yard." I am as deeply affected now as I was when I first experienced it, and I believe this is because, at its essence, the story is one of glimpsing God through the accomplishments and triumphs of a very special child.

- Have you seen God in the triumphs of your own children? Describe a situation and how you felt.
- Have your children faced and successfully endured difficult battles with illnesses, disabilities, or other challenges? If so, was God's love and healing power an important factor in the ultimate outcome?
- Have you adequately expressed your love, your joy, and your faith to your own children? If not, will you start now?

....

Chapter 7

GOD REVEALED . . .

IN THE WORKPLACE

....

Too often we try to totally separate our work life from our spiritual life, but I find that they can't be separated. For much of my life, my work consumed the vast majority of my time—and because God knew exactly where to find me, many of my encounters with Him occurred through work-related experiences.

The workplace also became the locus for much of my stress and anxiety. I often struggled with my purpose in life, the value of my chosen profession, the difficulty in bringing my faith to the workplace, and the challenge of realizing career success while remaining faithful to my values and beliefs. I suspect it's the same for many others.

In this chapter I share four work-related experiences in which God's involvement and presence seemed undeniable. As you search your memory for messages from God that you may have missed, I encourage you to focus on your work life. You may now realize that God was working alongside you. And as you engage yourself in the workplace in the future, don't do it alone. Invite God in through prayer as I have done daily during my thirty-five years in business. You're likely to discover, as I did, that you've had a very powerful business partner.

Pride and Congressional Sausage-Making

In 1984 I was the senior vice-president in charge of all product pricing and finance functions related to insurance products sold to individual retail customers for Maccabees Mutual Life Insurance Company in Southfield, Michigan. Because I managed multiple functions and made many difficult decisions almost every day, I relied heavily on my faith in God for guidance and was driven by a determination to do the right thing.

A very important consideration in product pricing was the level of corporate income taxes that would be paid by the company—a cost that ultimately had to be covered in the price of products sold to consumers. For many years, there had been a dispute in the industry over what would be fair and equitable taxes for mutual insurance companies and stock insurance companies—companies with quite different structures. The dispute had triggered the formation of several industry committees and task forces to find a solution that was acceptable to both types of companies.

In this complicated industry there is also a third category of nonprofit companies called *fraternal benefit societies*. Often set up by religious organizations to provide benefits to their members, these companies represent a very small percentage of the industry and are not subject to federal corporate income tax. However, a number of fraternal benefit societies have converted to mutual or stock insurance companies, which resulted in converting them into a tax-paying status. My company, Maccabees Mutual, fell into this category, as it had converted from a fraternal benefit society to a mutual company in March 1961.

In 1984, Congress finally made a serious effort to resolve this difficult taxation issue and enacted comprehensive tax law changes that spelled out specifically how the new law would determine annual taxes for mutual versus stock insurance companies. In response, many company executives, feeling the proposed law imposed an onerous tax burden on mutual life insurance companies, launched major, ultimately fruitless, battles and lobbying efforts before resigning themselves to higher taxes.

Though I had an interest in the emerging tax law, I had not actually read the text of the proposed legislation; instead, I had relied on summaries provided by my staff and by industry analysts and consultants. I understood the technical details of the new tax calculations and was concerned about the added cost it would create for my company. But I was even more concerned about our ability to pass those costs on to consumers without significantly damaging our competitive position in the wider market.

By mid-1984, when the proposed tax law had been passed by Congress and was in the joint Senate and House conference committee process for finalization, I decided to read the original legislation. "Hold all my calls," I told my assistant, as I carried the three-inch-thick printed draft into my office. "No interruptions for the whole afternoon." I shut my door and began to read.

I read as slowly as was necessary to understand the lengthy legalese. I read with total concentration. And, to my surprise, after several hours of this, I suddenly discovered something amazing: a provision in the law providing relief from this surplus tax for any mutual company that had converted from a fraternal benefit society to a mutual company in 1950. I had been reading to understand our fate; it had never occurred to me that there might be some relief for my own company in this legislation.

But there was a catch. Although the logic for the exemption made sense, it applied only to a single company in the industry—in spite of the fact that there were twenty companies in the nation that had converted from fraternal benefit societies to mutual companies. This was obviously one of those special "pork-barrel" provisions pushed through by an influential congressman or senator to benefit a company in his or her district. This was my first personal encounter with such a law, and I prickled at the injustice of it.

Something had to be done! I grabbed the phone and called the chief tax officer at Maccabees. "Jerry," I said, "is there any way this provision can be expanded to encompass all mutual companies that have previously converted from a fraternal benefit society?"

"Oh, Fred," he said, sounding tired. "It's way too late in the process to accomplish such a major change. The bill is already in conference committee!"

I was discouraged but not deterred. There had to be a way to do the right thing. Maccabees had no internal department of governmental affairs but it did have an external lobbyist. So I called him . . . only to receive the same response. "Isn't there something you can do?" I pleaded.

"Fred," he answered, "it really is too late, but I'll try contacting Representative Guy Vander Jagt's office. I believe he's a member of the conference committee and he's from Michigan. But don't get your hopes up; I suspect he will confirm that it's too late."

This was so unfair. Why had I not read the law earlier? I was embarrassed that I hadn't, but my discouragement gave way to even greater determination to see that the right thing was done.

Even before hearing back from the lobbyist, I quickly formed a team at Maccabees to research all other mutual companies that had historically converted from a fraternal benefit society. "I'd like you to estimate the potential federal revenue loss if the pork-barrel provision of the legislation were expanded to apply to all such companies," I told them.

In less than forty-eight hours, they identified all twenty companies and estimated potential lost revenues to be roughly $100 million per year. Although this number seemed large, it was actually extremely small in terms of total annual federal tax revenues. The team also determined the name of the company that was indirectly referenced in the existing pork-barrel provision and the name of the senator who successfully introduced the exemption on behalf of that company.

I personally called the top tax officers at all twenty of the other companies, and was I surprised at their response: none of them wanted to help in this effort; each was certain it was too late in the process to be successful; and many had already used up their political capital in lobbying for, or against, other provisions.

So I called the office of the senator who had introduced this provision. "Drop it if you know what's good for you," said the staff member I spoke to.

So this was the way Congress functions. It was disconcerting to say the least. And I was even more determined!

The research team I had assembled rapidly compiled materials making the theoretical case for similar tax relief for all twenty companies that had converted from fraternal benefit societies. Meanwhile, our lobbyist had contacted Rep. Vander Jagt, who surprisingly agreed to review and consider introducing our data and analysis. "We need it yesterday!" he declared.

Fortunately the work was done and our lobbyist delivered it the next morning to Rep. Vander Jagt—who informed us we would now have to wait. Until the law was released in its final form, we would not know what, if any, changes had been made to the final language.

It wasn't until a few weeks later that I received a copy of the final published law. Nervously I carried the thick book into my office, shut the door, and began to scour it for the appropriate section. There were at least two possible outcomes. The first—which seemed the most fair and appropriate—was for Congress to apply the exemption to all twenty similarly situated companies. If that were the outcome, I'd have accomplished my goal to do the right thing. The other possibility—not optimal, but certainly fairer than a single company's exemption—was to remove the original pork-barrel provision altogether.

Imagine my shock, thrill . . . and upset . . . at an outcome I'd never even considered. There in the final language was a new qualification on the original pork-barrel exemption that I'd discovered: now it applied to "mutual companies that had converted from fraternal benefit societies in 1950 or in March of 1961." Despite my determination to do the right thing, I had succeeded in achieving yet another pork-barrel provision for the benefit of my company and for Guy Vander Jagt's constituents. We had received the same preferential treatment afforded to the original sponsoring senator.

I was in an emotional whirlpool. On one hand, I was exhilarated and proud that my company would benefit from millions of dollars in reduced taxes annually for years to come, but how quickly pride turned to embarrassment and shame; I felt I had done something inappropriate, if not sinful. In my efforts to do the right thing, I'd become the major agent of an injustice. Add to that the fact that my company—and even many of my peers in the industry—exalted me for this remarkable "achievement."

What message was God sending me? I knew that my accomplishment would greatly enhance my career—but at what cost? Nothing was worth the inner turmoil and shame. If I had it to do over again, I'd push even harder. I would ensure equal treatment; I'd choose fairness over results that produced personal gain. Perhaps this was the message from God that I needed.

From then on, I watched out for business dealings that might be inconsistent with my underlying value system and ethics. I also caught myself often in moments of prideful egotism. I shared the story of the pork-barrel exemption often with many colleagues, friends, and employees, which gave me an opportunity to speak out against the unfair dealings in Congress. More importantly, however, it helped me emphasize the importance of humility in personal achievement and integrity in business—and that lesson was a positive testimony to many friends and colleagues.

.... *For Reflection* ....
For it is not the one who commends himself who is approved,
but the one whom the Lord commends.

2 Corinthians 10:18

Firsthand experience with the lawmaking process in Washington can be both enlightening and shocking. Plunged into the center of it, the greatest business success in my career came through a process that both embarrassed and astounded me. It also revealed my own inclination to experience sinful pride.

This difficult situation was so unlikely and such a long shot that I felt certain God was involved in its orchestration—not only for my benefit, but also for the benefit of thousands of Maccabees' policyholders. However, my immediate reaction to this remarkable success, one of great pride, was quickly overcome by shame and guilt. The lasting message from God was to avoid pride, to be on the alert for unethical business dealings and practices, and to set an example for others by demonstrating ethical behavior and integrity in all of my dealings.

Do you occasionally get caught up in your own successes and demonstrate pride or even hubris? The Bible has literally hundreds of verses addressing the sin of pride. In most cases the emphasis is on the fact that pride leads us to feel superior and then to behave in an arrogant or condescending way to our fellow men and women. Think back on how often you have fallen into this trap.

It is appropriate to enjoy a sense of accomplishment, especially when we recognize and thank God for His role in producing results aligned with our own spiritual gifts and divine calling. Such actions and accomplishments please God—and, as Paul indicates in his second letter to the Corinthians, commendations from the Lord are far superior to commendations of self.

Lunch with a President

One Monday morning in 1995, while going over my schedule for the week, I noticed a curious calendar item for the next day: "Lunch with the President." I couldn't remember making an appointment with any corporate presidents. Why hadn't my assistant noted the name of the president's company? "Can you please follow up?" I asked her. "I need to know who I'm meeting."

Minutes later, looking flustered and embarrassed, our public relations officer rushed into my office. "I am so sorry," she told me. "I really should have notified you about this meeting ahead of time. You are eating lunch with *the* president. President Gerald Ford."

You could have knocked me over with a feather.

As mentioned in the earlier story of my encounter with President Clinton, New York Life was the sole sponsor of the PBS television series *The Presidents*; as a result, I had the honor of meeting several former presidents of the United States. This was the first such opportunity and I looked forward to it with great anticipation, wondering if I might even get the opportunity to speak directly with President Ford.

As vice-chairman, I was third in command at New York Life, but assumed there would be perhaps fifty or sixty top officers and guests at the lunch. With a group that size, I figured our chairman and our president would be seated with President Ford and that I would be entertaining other visitors in the president's entourage at a separate table.

About an hour before the luncheon the next day, the public relations officer reappeared at my door. "Oh, Fred," she said, "did I tell you that you will be hosting the luncheon today?" She reminded me that both the chairman and the president of New York Life were out of the office.

"Boy you're full of surprises, aren't you? I'm glad you didn't make me nervous by giving me any time to think about this! By the way, how many New York Life executives will attend?"

"Only three," she told me. Only five altogether would attend the luncheon: President Ford, presidential historian Hugh Sidey, and three of us from New York Life—the human resources officer, the public relations officer, and *me*.

Needless to say, I panicked. I'd be expected to make opening remarks! And then carry the conversation! As I'd done daily throughout my business career, I paused to ask God to help me prepare for the meeting and to guide my thoughts, words, and actions.

I tried to think of some questions for President Ford. Realizing my knowledge of his term was limited, I quickly asked for help from two of my direct reports at New York Life who were not only great conversationalists but were also well-versed on recent history.

Nervously I scribbled some opening remarks welcoming the president, providing some background on New York Life and its involvement in the PBS production, and expressing our gratitude for the honor of his visit. I constructed a few questions that were suggested by my two employees, and then I pondered what I wanted to ask.

I'd always had a burning interest in President John F. Kennedy's assassination. Over the years I had read everything I could get my hands on relating to it, including much of the encyclopedic twenty-six–volume report of the Warren Commission. Volume 5 of that report contained the transcript of a meeting that took place with Jack Ruby (who killed Lee Harvey Oswald, Kennedy's alleged assassin) in his Dallas prison cell; the meeting was attended by President Ford, who was then a U.S. congressman and a member of the Warren Commission, and Lee Rankin, the commission's general counsel.

In the transcript, Ruby indicated he knew much more than he was revealing about the assassination but insisted he didn't feel safe in Dallas; he asked to be taken to Washington, where he promised to reveal what he knew. Inexplicably, the federal government—even with its vast resources—did not take Ruby to Washington. Instead, they left him in the Dallas prison, where he died of cancer a few months later. I was eager to ask President Ford why he didn't have Ruby transferred to Washington.

I had always been fascinated with Ruby and his potential role in the assassination. There was much conjecture about Ruby's association with the Mafia and his possible prior relationship with Lee Harvey Oswald. Many thought the killing of Oswald was far more than the crazed act of a bereaved citizen seeking revenge for the president's assassination. And some journalists and authors felt the Warren Commission wanted to rush to judgment against Oswald as the sole assassin, preferring not to hear any evidence to the contrary. To be able to ask this question of a key governmental player who had actually interviewed Ruby face-to-face was a Kennedy assassination buff's dream—and I was ready and eager to pose the question at the first opportune moment.

The initial luncheon conversation went well. I made my planned opening remarks relatively smoothly without the use of notes. And throughout the next two hours, President Ford was extremely gracious and congenial. He spoke freely about his years in the White House, about his family, and about Betty Ford's formation of an alcohol treatment center. The time passed quickly for all five of us in the room as we listened to "the inside story" from a man who once held the most powerful office in the world. And throughout it all, I watched for my opportunity to jump in with my burning question.

But just when I thought the perfect time had come, historian Hugh Sidey preempted me. "Mr. President," he said, "as the only surviving member of the Warren Commission, what are your thoughts now about the single-bullet theory?" Knowing that many of those familiar with the assassination believed there was more than one assassin, I almost breathlessly awaited President Ford's response.

Before Mr. Sidey asked the question, the president had been quite relaxed, leaning back in his chair and talking as if he were among close friends at a country club. But as soon as he heard that question, all that changed. Leaning forward, he glared at Mr. Sidey and, pounding his fist on the table three times, declared, "That Oswald was a lunatic! He did it alone, and I never saw any evidence to the contrary!"

After observing his reaction and out of respect for one of the most honored guests ever to visit New York Life, I immediately realized that it would be extremely unwise to pose my probing question. I had missed my opportunity—but I don't regret my decision to move on to less controversial matters. It seemed to me that—just as I had asked—God was indeed guiding my thoughts and my words through the Holy Spirit.

The discussion returned easily to a more congenial tone for the next half hour. During the final minutes of the luncheon, I never once reconsidered raising the question about Ruby. It seemed obvious that President Ford's term on the Warren Commission was a source of some stress for him, and I surmised that he had often been asked questions about his role and his opinion about its published conclusions. Perhaps even then, more than thirty years after the assassination, he felt obligated to fully support the Warren Commission conclusions irrespective of his possible personal doubts.

None of us wanted this delightful experience to end, and we were astonished when the president looked at his watch and apologized for keeping *us* so long. "Thank you," he said, "for the delicious meal and your hospitality."

I made some brief closing remarks, thanking the president for joining us and for providing us with some fascinating insights into the life and challenges of the presidency. It was my first encounter with a United States president, and I was surprised by how comfortable I felt in his presence. I thanked God that this meeting had gone so well, that I had presided so comfortably, and that I had not embarrassed myself or New York Life.

When President Ford died some years later, it occurred to me that he went to his grave with very few people being aware of his jailhouse interview with Jack Ruby. Fewer still ever would have had the opportunity to ask him about it. While I would love to know his answer to my million-dollar question, I am grateful that God was with me that afternoon and had spared me the embarrassment of antagonizing an honored guest and potentially ruining an incredible experience.

·············· *For Reflection* ··············

Desire without knowledge is not good— how much more will hasty feet miss the way!

Proverbs 19:2

There are different kinds of working, but in all of them and in everyone it is the same God at work. Now to each one the manifestation of the Spirit is given or the common good. To one there is given through the Spirit a message of wisdom, to another a message of knowledge by means of the same Spirit.

1 Corinthians 12:6–8

. . . .

Few people ever get the opportunity to spend time with a current or former president of the United States. Given that opportunity, one would want to thoroughly prepare for the experience. I had little time for preparation, but it seems that God was faithful in answering my brief prayers for assistance. God must have been watching over me with particular energy and interest, because His intervention was the only thing that saved me from making a very foolish mistake. Hugh Sidey, as a presidential historian who had interviewed every living president during his career, often posed challenging questions that provoked negative responses. For Sidey, the risks were low and the president's reactions almost uneventful, the experience being a part of Sidey's professional research; but for me, a representative of the company who had been charged with overseeing a pleasant and hospitable discussion, the risks were great. As in Proverbs 19, my inquisitiveness and desire almost caused my hasty feet to miss the way.

I hadn't thought through these considerations in advance of Sidey's question to the president, and, in hindsight, the truth of Paul's message in the first letter to the Corinthians has never been more meaningful to me. It was indeed the wisdom given *through* the Spirit that guided my actions.

That lunch with the president was not the only time I felt God's nearness while working—during my business career, I prayed brief prayers many times daily and always felt God's presence through the Holy Spirit, not just in the workplace, but in all aspects of my life.

Do you speak to God daily, or do you instead reserve such prayer time for Sunday worship or devotions? Are you uncomfortable asking for God's help in the workplace? I would encourage you to recognize that in every minute and hour of every day of the week, God is with you.

Trusting God to See Us through Failures

In the mid-1990s, New York Life became aware of an opportunity at the Federal National Mortgage Association (Fannie Mae). With more than $1 trillion in assets, it was the largest financial institution in the world, and we had the chance to offer life insurance to millions of consumers who had obtained mortgages through this agency.

The greatest source of financial risk to the corporate profits of Fannie Mae occurred when the primary income producer in the household died and the mortgage went unpaid. To protect against this risk and dramatically diminish expected losses, Fannie Mae decided to offer a life insurance program to the homeowners (i.e., the mortgagors), which thereby would result in the dual benefit of lower-cost mortgages for all of the homeowners and greater profitability for Fannie Mae.

Under this program, Fannie Mae would pay the entire insurance premium. There would be no added cost to the homeowner. At the time of death of the homeowner, the death benefit payment from the insurance company would be made directly to the Fannie Mae organization thereby paying off the outstanding loan balance. To make this particularly attractive to consumers, additional levels of insurance coverage were available, and any death benefits in excess of the outstanding loan balance would be paid to the beneficiary designated by the borrower—in most cases a spouse and/or other family members.

It was a win-win situation. It was a phenomenal benefit for consumers, offering free coverage; it provided default protection and added profits for Fannie Mae; and it had the potential of almost instantly boosting New York Life's revenues and profits to unprecedented levels. I felt it was a true gift from God for everyone, and the sequence of events leading up to New York Life's involvement seemed providential.

New York Life learned of this opportunity through a consultant who was aware of our reputation, product, and administrative capabilities and who had high-level contacts at Fannie Mae. He arranged for me to make a presentation in a private morning meeting with top Fannie Mae executives in Washington, D.C. Over breakfast that morning, the consultant briefed me on the scope and intent of the project and made me aware of some internal issues at Fannie Mae that were causing significant frustration among senior management. That knowledge enabled me to quickly determine the areas where New York Life provided a strong competitive edge as well as the ways in which we could instantly address many of Fannie Mae's greatest frustrations.

Because of the strength and reputation of New York Life and its proven capability to administer a project of this magnitude, we were chosen over several competing companies to administer the entire program. Even before my visit, the Fannie Mae board of directors had approved an expenditure of nearly $5 billion in initial premiums; after my visit, administration of the project was awarded to New York Life based on our reputation and capabilities as highlighted in my presentation. In that presentation I focused not only on New York Life's product and administrative capability but also provided a specific example of our creativity and adaptability in dealing with a large class-action lawsuit for more than 3.8 million claimants. Having promised to assign the most talented product and administrative people to this project, I immediately assembled the team and sent them to Washington the very next day.

Together, the New York Life team and the Fannie Mae team began to develop the product and implement the program on a very aggressive timetable. There was renewed energy and confidence at Fannie Mae.

To put the magnitude of this project into proper perspective, New York Life could expect an initial premium of around $2 billion and ongoing annual premiums of another $0.5 billion. This single project would roughly double the size of New York Life's revenues from new sales and would instantly thrust the company into the number-one market share position for life insurance sales. At the time there were over 1,000 life insurance companies in the United States and to be ranked number one in new sales would have been a remarkable achievement. Over time, this deal with FNMA would also increase the overall number of customers and the overall level of total revenues by thirty to forty percent. We stood to gain strong profitability at relatively low risk and with little competition. And consumers throughout the socioeconomic spectrum would benefit greatly.

This had to be a gift from God. With His guidance in dealing with all emerging issues and obstacles, the deal was shaping up to be the most significant business arrangement in which I had ever participated. I prayed daily for the success of this venture and continuously thanked God for the opportunity to positively impact so many lives through my chosen profession.

As the project progressed, however, many challenges and difficulties surfaced. The entire deal was highly dependent on pending legislation in Congress that provided very favorable federal borrowing rates for Fannie Mae. The insurance program in particular was recognized as highly beneficial, and Congress seemed to support the pending legislation. Even though passage of the legislation seemed assured, New York Life launched an aggressive effort to lobby key members of the Senate Finance Committee and the House Ways and Means Committee. I personally visited Washington and spoke to several committee members; all of the lobbied legislators expressed support. In addition, Fannie Mae was perhaps the most powerful lobby group in Washington and always had achieved its legislative goals.

As the bill approached a vote in the Senate Finance Committee, preparation to launch the program took on epic proportions. The effort involved a very large team of people from Fannie Mae, New York Life, and several other participating companies.

The evening before I was to leave on vacation to Europe, the Senate Finance Committee held its final meeting on the bill. In an 11 p.m. call from New York Life's Chief Government Affairs Officer Jessie Colgate, I was told that the bill had passed and we were "home free." Jubilant, I praised God for facilitating this seemingly miraculous sequence of events. What a marvelous way to launch my European vacation!

But my joy was short-lived. Just thirty minutes later, Jessie called with the devastating news that the approval had been reversed. A chief staff member—one I had personally met with a few days earlier—had pleaded with the committee to retract its approval because of the perceived unfair advantage given to Fannie Mae in the federal funds borrowing rate. After a proposed amendment to remove the favored status for Fannie Mae, the committee reversed itself. Fannie Mae lost the financial proposition and the entire concept was destroyed.

Attempts to restore this provision over the next few days, while I was on vacation, failed; the project was officially on hold. For several weeks the New York Life team looked for ways to restructure the program in a way that would remain attractive to Fannie Mae and to the participating insurance companies but could come up with nothing. What appeared to be my biggest career success had become my biggest failure.

Three months later at a White House reception sponsored by Fannie Mae's chairman, many of the key players from both New York Life and Fannie Mae discussed the unfortunate outcome of this situation. We concluded there was no way to salvage a desirable product and program without the necessary legislation.

If God's hand was in the failure of the Fannie Mae deal, I hadn't figured out why. It can be very difficult to understand such disappointments but I firmly believed there was a reason for what happened. I now know that He had not deserted us and, in fact, was heavily involved in the amazing events that happened next.

As soon as they returned to New York, team members—discouraged but not defeated—started discussing how to take this product concept to a new market. Bob Hebron, the key New York Life architect who had worked on the Fannie Mae deal structure, had an idea. An emerging national accounting standard was surfacing that would impact banks in particular. Bob started working on a product design for life insurance to be sold on the lives of bank officers and employees; as with the Fannie Mae plan, the policies would be owned by the banks and would also name the banks as beneficiaries that would receive the death payments. Over the long term, death benefits from the plan would in effect fund the large new liability on the banks' books. Because of the tax advantages of life insurance and the relatively small initial premiums, this was considered a highly effective means for the banks to fund the added liability that otherwise would have been much higher in current costs on their financial statements. It appeared that God was still solidly with us, inspiring this new concept. The only disappointment for me personally was that this arrangement had a far less direct impact on consumers. Only indirectly and over the long term would the benefits of this insurance purchase inure to the benefit of the banks' customers.

In partnership with a national marketing organization, New York Life put together a plan design that was marketed to virtually every large bank in the United States and many medium and small banks over the ensuing seven or eight years. Ultimately the amount of premium revenue New York Life received from these bank-owned life insurance sales—a total of more than $4 billion—equaled or exceeded what would have been received through Fannie Mae. New York Life rapidly moved to the number-one market share position despite the failure to execute the FNMA deal.

In the end, the tremendous effort we invested in the Fannie Mae experience was not wasted, and both New York Life and the banking industry benefited enormously from working together to find and meet a market need. Under God's guidance a great concept was conceived, and despite the disappointment of the Fannie Mae failure, His help resulted in a positive outcome that benefitted many banks and, indirectly, their large number of customers.

.... *For Reflection* ....

Trust in the Lord with all your heart and lean not on your own understanding; in all your ways submit to him, and he will make your paths straight.

Proverbs 3:5–6

One of the largest and most exciting projects I ever worked on was the life insurance program to insure millions whose mortgages were guaranteed by Fannie Mae. After things came together in such a miraculous way, imagine my frustration when the effort was thwarted at the eleventh hour by failed legislation in Congress. I was so sure God had been in on it from the beginning—and, as it turned out, He wasn't finished yet.

Only with His help did we ultimately achieve huge success. A creative but failed project in one design (Fannie Mae-owned life insurance) led to a repackaged and successful project in another design (bank-owned life insurance).

Have you ever prayed earnestly in your life for desired outcomes that never materialized? Have you puzzled over why God would not step in during your times of greatest need to facilitate something that seemed beneficial to all concerned—and that even seemed a means of glorifying God? Have you trusted in God only to feel He ignored or deserted you? If you have remained faithful and yet you find yourself at times feeling disappointed or abandoned, you certainly aren't alone.

My experience encourages me and might encourage you to remain prayerful and trusting of our God. The one common denominator in all of this work was that I prayed to and relied on God in both the failed project and in the successful project. The end result was highly successful even though it wasn't the one all of us at New York Life and Fannie Mae had envisioned.

I believe faithfulness, trust, and reliance on God were ultimately rewarded. We must always trust that the most beneficial outcome will ultimately prevail because of God's timing and God's faithfulness. I love the wisdom books of the Bible, particularly the succinct and wisdom-filled verses of Proverbs. As stated in Proverbs 3:5–6, we shouldn't lean on our own understanding, but rather submit to God, who will make our paths straight.

Impacting the Lives of Others

In college, I majored in mathematics, and when I left teaching, a career as an actuary seemed appropriate given my educational training. Actuaries are experts who apply their knowledge of mathematics, probability, statistics, and risk theory to insurance-related problems involving future uncertainty. It's a highly technical career, and although I knew it would be quite a change from teaching mathematics, which I had greatly enjoyed, I took to it with interest.

During the 1980s, I was in various positions at Maccabees Mutual Life Insurance Company. Though my training was as an actuary, I quickly moved into more generalized financial management as the corporate CFO and later was placed in charge of all functions related to the company's life insurance, disability insurance, and annuity lines of business. Before leaving the company in 1991, I had advanced to the second highest-ranking executive position at the company, reporting directly to the chief executive officer, Jules Pallone.

I'd loved my previous career as a teacher, and my role at Maccabees was very different and more technical. Although I felt that by changing careers I had lost some of the ability to impact young lives, I felt fulfilled and I could see that God was using my newly developed executive skills to positively manage and lead the company's employees.

I felt a strong affinity for my colleagues who were engaged in the highly complex work of actuarial experts, not only at my company in Michigan, but elsewhere in the insurance industry. I was truly grateful that my actuarial training and background had been such an excellent launch pad for an interesting and successful executive career. Because of that gratitude, I wanted to give back to the profession, to stay abreast of important industry issues, and to remain in contact with my actuarial colleagues. So I volunteered on a number of industry committees; I also went through a series of leadership positions in the Michigan Actuarial Society, ultimately serving as its president in 1986.

In the year of my presidency, I was invited to Central Michigan University (CMU) by the math department to speak to students and faculty about the actuarial profession. I discussed the variety of strong career opportunities for actuaries and the rigorous study regimen required in achieving the exam-based professional designations of Associate of the Society of Actuaries (ASA) and the higher-level Fellow of the Society of Actuaries (FSA). Even for superior college graduates, achieving the FSA designation required well more than five years of intense post-graduate study and the passing of multiple examinations.

The presentation went well—reminding me how much I loved teaching and how I still desired to positively impact the lives of young students. Many questions were raised by both the faculty and the math students, and I felt good about introducing the profession. Maybe some of the young people would now consider entering the industry and I hoped that the university might establish a curriculum to help educate them on some of the more difficult mathematical concepts.

Following that visit, I didn't maintain any further contact with the university, its faculty, or its students. Nonetheless, I felt good about having donated my time in this way that allowed me to "give back" to the profession.

After I moved on to New York Life in 1992, my career flourished. I enjoyed annual promotions similar to those I had enjoyed at Maccabees, but New York Life was a Fortune 100 company—by most measures at least twenty-five times larger than Maccabees. But despite my intense work schedule, I remained committed to some level of volunteer work within the industry.

Over the subsequent years, I maintained only occasional contact with many of my friends from Maccabees. In 2005, when I was the president of New York Life, the president of the Michigan Actuarial Society wrote to ask if I might be available in July 2005 to speak to their society meeting in Ann Arbor. As it turned out, I was planning to return to Michigan to attend the Major League Baseball All-Star Game, which was being played in Detroit that year—and the society dinner just happened to be scheduled for the night before the game. "Yes!" I replied. "I would love to attend and to speak to the group."

How many members of the society would show up in mid-July? I recalled that dinner meetings held on Monday nights typically attracted only thirty or forty people. Nonetheless, I put a lot of thought into my presentation, which covered brief background information on New York Life and my analysis of the key issues facing the insurance industry. To my absolute delight, there was a huge audience, and a significant percentage of them were former colleagues of mine from Maccabees. What a gratifying and wonderful reunion. And to top it off, my former boss and mentor, the retired Maccabees CEO and Chairman of the Board Jules Pallone, drove two hours from his home to attend.

But the most moving moment came before I was even introduced to speak. Although there were more than a hundred attendees, the moderator asked each of them to briefly introduce himself or herself by name and company affiliation. I listened carefully to get a feel for the background and experience of my audience, and adjusted a few of my remarks accordingly. But God touched me deeply when the introductions finally ended at a table of nine young people and one older gentleman at the back of the room.

"I am on the faculty of Central Michigan University," announced the older gentleman, standing. "And I'd like you to meet my students." He went on to introduce all nine—all of whom had driven well more than two hours from Mt. Pleasant, Michigan, to attend this dinner. "It is an honor for all of us to be here," he told me. "We came in order to personally thank you—as the founder of the actuarial studies program at CMU." He mentioned my visit in 1986 and how that presentation had triggered activity on the part of the faculty to learn more about the profession and to then establish an academic program in actuarial science. What a success the program was, he said, reporting the number of students who had entered the profession over the years and were now working in the actuarial field in Michigan and elsewhere in the United States.

Until that moment I had almost totally forgotten about my visit to their campus nearly twenty years earlier. I didn't deserve the title of "founder." Nonetheless, I was moved by this recognition, wondering why God chose *now* to remind me of this distant and seemingly inconsequential bygone event.

In my busy schedule as president of New York Life, I was asked to speak on the evening before a day that I had already planned to be in Detroit. Yes, it was wonderful to see my friends and colleagues from Maccabees, especially my dear friend and mentor Jules Pallone, but I felt certain God was behind this for a bigger purpose. As I contemplated that question, it became clear: I was just beginning a self-assessment of the passions I would follow into retirement. Two years later, I would retire early, at the age of fifty-nine, in order to pursue several such passions. This providential moment in 2005 was important in collecting and assessing my thoughts on how, in retirement, I could most effectively impact the lives of young people and, more specifically, how I might act on my lifelong love for education and teaching.

Shortly after the experience in Michigan, I began to construct a curriculum for a business school course in executive management and leadership that I would market to three universities, all of which were eager to hire me as an adjunct professor.

The Michigan experience also revealed to me the unanticipated but enduring benefits that can result from volunteer work and other acts of kindness. In addition to teaching the business school course, I was determined to remain active in volunteering my time and talents to the profession and its young, aspiring executives. Since retirement I have been actively mentoring four such individuals pursuing careers in management.

The enormous personal satisfaction from these post-retirement activities may never have materialized if it hadn't been for that poignant and surprising moment in Ann Arbor at the Michigan Actuarial Society dinner. Many of the attendees later sent me notes and emails indicating how much my remarks had educated and enriched their business knowledge. What they couldn't possibly have known is how much the experience contributed to a far more meaningful retirement for me.

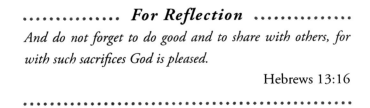

·············· *For Reflection* ··············
And do not forget to do good and to share with others, for
with such sacrifices God is pleased.

Hebrews 13:16

When we give unselfishly of ourselves, when we reach out and help others through volunteerism, we often don't realize the far-reaching impact it can have. Even small, single-event gestures of kindness can impact multiple lives over an extended period.

I was reminded of this at the dinner meeting in Ann Arbor some twenty years after I had donated only a half day of my time to promote the actuarial profession to students and faculty at Central Michigan University. God was reminding me that my passion for impacting young lives was paying off in ways I never dreamed possible.

God knew I was struggling with my own retirement plans at that moment, and through this experience He was speaking to me about my future in a way I had not anticipated at all. Following retirement, some of my most gratifying experiences have come from my actuarial volunteer work, my teaching of business school students, and my mentoring of aspiring executives.

Do you have a sense of gratitude for your many blessings that inspires you to sacrifice some of your time to "give back"? Giving back may involve a host of different kinds of volunteer work—church programs, missionary work, or many types of community service. I can assure you that you will find it very rewarding and gratifying.

More importantly, the benefits go beyond you and even those you serve. As the writer of the letter to the Hebrews reminded us, when we do good and share with others our sacrifices are pleasing to God.

Chapter 7 Exercises

It seems that many well-intending, practicing Christians, struggle with bringing God and their faith into the workplace. Since the early days of my career, I have spoken to God and relied upon His guidance in the workplace daily. I must somewhat ashamedly admit, however, that I was more cautious about sharing the specifics of my faith in a workplace in which I had a leadership role and my employees represented virtually every imaginable faith tradition and denomination. Nonetheless, God was with me daily and the stories of chapter 7 reflect some of the more notable examples.

Avoiding Pride

In the story "Pride and Congressional Sausage-Making," God's hand seemed to be guiding me to a remarkable legislative achievement that significantly benefited my company in what could only be labeled a "pork-barrel" corporate tax provision. I struggled mightily: first, with the pride of achieving such an accomplishment, and then with the guilt of doing so for my personal gain and the benefit of only one single company—my company.

- Have you felt extreme pride in some of your own accomplishments?
- Do you struggle with the biblical admonitions against the sin of pride?
- Is it a sin to feel proud of our children and of others? Is there a better way than "pride" to express this feeling?
- Can you elaborate on the Bible passages you know of that characterize pride as sin (e.g. Mark 7:20–23; Proverbs 8:13; Romans 12:3) and tell us how you would interpret them?

Trusting God in Our Failures

In what we perceive to be devastating failures, we often lament that God simply wasn't by our side and didn't answer our prayers. Nonetheless, we often learn much and grow immeasurably from the experiences that we call "failures." In the story "Trusting God to See Us through Failures," I describe one of my most disappointing work experiences—leading a dedicated team that worked tirelessly on a major project only to see it thwarted by negative legislative action in the eleventh hour. In short order, however, applying what we learned from the experience, the team executed an equally impressive completed project. I'm convinced God was indeed in both the initial failure and the ultimate success.

- Can you identify something that was very important to you, which you initially failed miserably to achieve?
- Did you believe God had abandoned you in your efforts?
- Did anything good occur as a result of your perceived failure; did you in any way realize a later benefit from the earlier experience?
- On reflection, do you see that God's hand may have been guiding you more than you initially realized?

Touching Lives

How fitting it is to end chapter 7 and the stories of this book with an example of how our acts of kindness can so positively— even unknowingly—impact other lives. In the final story, "Impacting the Lives of Others," I learned nearly twenty years after a presentation I had made—a presentation designed to give back to my profession—that it had resulted in the establishment of a college degree program that impacted hundreds of students' lives. Our actions, our words, and our testimonies can powerfully touch the lives of many individuals in ways we never anticipated.

- Has anyone ever told you years later that something you once did or said had a strong positive influence on them?
- Did such an experience ever relate to expressions of your faith or actions consistent with your faith?
- Can you think of times you held back for fear of how people might respond if you proactively expressed your faith in public?
- Will you resolve to watch for opportunities to share your faith in the future and act upon them? In so doing, you will please God and positively touch many lives.

Chapter 8

RECEIVING AND RESPONDING TO GOD'S MESSAGES

Committing my experiences to writing has catapulted me into many hours of deep reflection: What has been God's role in my life? How has His presence been constant—regardless of whether I recognized it at the time? What have I learned about God, about myself, and about coping with my hectic lifestyle? How can I, as well as others, be attentive to our relationship with God, no matter what the distractions?

Despite my failures and shortcomings, I have been richly blessed. Perhaps my daily life has been conducted at a more frantic pace than most people's, but it is clear to me that increasingly more Americans are falling into the same traps I've fallen into.

I have had a constant desire to succeed in worldly terms, to advance my business career, and to boost my socioeconomic status. At the same time, I've longed to balance the family and spiritual dimensions of my life. The actual result of the journey wasn't quite what I intended:

I experienced career success but that success came at the expense of successes in my spiritual development and in my family relationships.

My priorities were often upside down, and I have regrets. I regret that I still have not quite achieved the balance I've hoped for. I have given time to my family and to my church but it hasn't always been focused or adequate, nor has it always made effective use of the spiritual gifts God bestowed upon me.

This book began as a simple written account of my experiences and encounters with God; it was intended for the benefit of my family. As I wrote, however, it evolved into something far greater. It has become a ministry of sorts to include not only the book but a website and social media accounts that have expanded dramatically to reach a very large audience. They continue to grow and have proved to be far more powerful than I ever anticipated.

So now, after a long and successful career in business, God has helped me find ways in which I can more effectively touch other lives and better utilize my spiritual gifts. The exercise of writing this book has enabled me to pursue fruitful and meaningful service to the Lord in what I hope will be many remaining years on this earth. I hope and pray that as you read this book and join me on this journey, your future will also be enriched.

Your age is completely irrelevant. You may be long into retirement or just starting your career; you may be newly married or a doting grandparent; you may be a young single person, never married, or a divorced or widowed man or woman. The important thing is what you realize about your own relationship with God. No matter how old you are or what your circumstances, you can learn from your experiences as I have learned from mine, and draw closer to God as I have. As the stories in this book trigger recollections of similar or related encounters you have had with God, I hope you will be better prepared to hear from God in the future and to respond appropriately. I pray that reading this book will enable you to learn more about yourself, more about God, and more about how you can more effectively serve Him.

As you have read each story and thoughtfully considered the questions and prompts in the "For Reflection" sections, you have probably constructed your own list of providential encounters with God. With your list in mind, I now ask you to reflect on three primary questions:

1. How can you be well prepared to experience or hear from God in the future?
2. What have your encounters revealed about the nature of God?
3. How might you respond to messages or guidance from God?

To better facilitate your personal reflections and responses to these questions, I'd like to share some of my own conclusions and observations about these three questions.

Preparing to Hear from God

This book includes thirty-one experiences in my life when I felt I encountered God and felt His presence and influence, but there have been many, many more. In some cases God was answering prayers—on His divine timetable, not always on mine. At other times He was simply watching over me, guiding me, or protecting me. My story is one of God's remarkable grace and blessings manifested throughout my life.

To be honest, there were times when I felt my prayers weren't answered and God was nowhere to be found. In hindsight, however, it was weeks, months, or even years before I realized that what seemed to be inadequate or undesirable outcomes were actually part of God's divine plan. Even so, I know that many faithful people suffer horribly during their lives from the loss of loved ones, from physical ailments, from poverty, from oppression, or from other forms of deprivation and abuse. I don't know why God doesn't seem to answer their prayers on a timely basis. As indicated earlier in the book, I have some tough questions for God when I get to the other side.

Human suffering affects us all. No one is exempt. Death touches all of us during our lifetimes, and the death of loved ones is an inevitable and important part of all of our lives. Suffering can, and often does, test our faith. But it can also buttress our faith.

All humans experience the emotional pleasures of love, personal accomplishment, and joy while at times enduring the pain of disappointment, frustration, anger, or depression. I believe God has designed and created the body and mind to allow for this broad range of joy and suffering. One of the mysteries *and* marvels of God's human creation is that our ability to withstand pain and suffering may actually enhance and intensify periods of joy and happiness.

The key revelation for me is that God is there to provide hope for those who have become severely debilitated by pain and suffering. It is through faith in Him, reliance on Him, and prayer to Him that God reveals Himself to many with His healing powers. The personal testimonies that result from examples of divine healing strengthen the church and the body of believers.

My personal experiences and observations convince me that God is here to see us through these difficult times—to provide us with the strength to overcome and move on. This is true despite the fact that the inveterate and nagging question of *Why me?* may never be adequately answered.

The stories I have recounted are largely about the triumphs and joys I attribute to God's role in my life. God was there for me in times of need and to provide wisdom and guidance in all aspects of my life.

Though I feel blessed in so many ways, I have also faced difficult times. Those struggles are often implied or even referenced in the stories, but I don't always dwell on the extent of my suffering. Early in our marriage, Sue and I struggled financially, I suffered from debilitating migraine headaches, I lost my best friend to the war in Vietnam, Sue and I suffered years of infertility, I often felt my job was in jeopardy, I worried intensely about my son's depression, I often felt controlled and overwhelmed in the workplace, and I lost my parents and other loved ones to relatively early deaths.

This book doesn't focus on my challenges and struggles because I want instead to highlight and rejoice in the way God revealed Himself when I needed Him. Throughout my life, I've consistently relied on the power of God. My reliance was born of the strong faith I developed during the mystical experience when I was twelve, a faith that has sustained me throughout my youth, my early adult life, my working years, and now my retirement.

For me, that faith and my faithfulness have always been a rich blessing from God. I am often reminded of and can relate to chapter 11 of the book of Hebrews, which alludes to example after example of biblical heroes who maintained their faith until death and were commended and rewarded by God. I feel I must be forever vigilant in my stewardship of the gift of faith given to me. As Hebrews 6:11 warns, "Without faith it is impossible to please God, because anyone who comes to Him must believe that He exists and that He rewards those who earnestly seek Him."

A rich life of prayer has also helped prepare me to receive messages and blessings from God. In good times and bad, I have prayed short and simple prayers to God multiple times daily, and I have always attempted to intercede on behalf of friends and family in my daily prayer routine. Like the Psalmist in the Psalm 116:1, my gratitude for a God who has been there for me in my times of need encourages me to call out to Him often:

> I love the LORD, for He heard my voice;
> He heard my cry for mercy.
> Because He turned His ear to me,
> I will call on Him as long as I live.

But even with an unfailing faith and a strong life of prayer, I often missed God's messages or didn't recognize His presence in an important encounter. Faithfulness and prayerfulness have made me receptive to messages from God but I also need to be watchful. I am reminded and reassured by the wisdom of Proverbs 8:34–35:

> Blessed are those who listen to me,
> watching daily at my doors,
> waiting at my doorway.
> For those who find me find life
> and receive favor from the LORD.

My prescription for preparing yourself to hear God's messages and experience God's divine work in your life is this: Steadfastly endure your own suffering and pain in the knowledge that God is with you and will provide relief. Pray daily for your own needs and for those of others in your family and circle of friends and acquaintances, and watch for God's answers to prayer and His guidance and direction to you.

Put simply, the best way to prepare to hear from God is to remain *faithful*, *prayerful*, and *watchful*, no matter what challenges you face.

Discoveries about God's Nature

As a result of the experiences I share in the stories of this book, I have learned much about God's nature and character. It's important to recognize that my learning process, like yours, is never-ending, and I continue to learn more from my daily walk with Him. Reading the submissions of hundreds of people who have visited my website and shared their own revelatory encounters with God has also helped me better understand Him, and their testimonies of God's activity and revealed presence in their lives are an added revelation and a blessing to me.

When I was young, I struggled with the fact that I couldn't physically "see" God or literally "hear" His voice. It made me wonder if others who claimed to have heard or seen God were lying or delusional. Worse, I wondered if somehow God had given me a "glimpse" of Him when I was twelve and had then left my side for good.

I no longer believe that is the case. The experiences I share in this book have taught me that an apparently invisible and elusive God has, in a strange but wonderful way, encouraged me to learn more and to seek Him more earnestly. The comfort of daily prayers and the realization that He is with me always and is interceding in my life has fortified rather than challenged my faith. The irony of a God who can't be seen but reveals Himself through the experiences of our lives has been a revelation to me, and it is what inspired me to write this book.

As I attempt to describe the nature of God, I realize what a daunting task that is and I recognize the limitations of my ability to adequately articulate such a description. In prayerfully and thoughtfully making this effort, I have drawn on numerous sources. Those sources include what I have read about God in the Bible, what I learned during my four years of graduate study in divinity school, what I recall about my mystical adolescent experience, and what I learned in all of my subsequent encounters with God, some of which I have related in this book.

As I attempt to relive and recreate my emotional response when I have most palpably felt God's presence in my life, I find that the most succinct and simplest way to describe God's nature is the expression *God is love*. When God was closest to me, when God was undeniably impacting my life, when God was reaching out to guide me or to carry me through difficult times, when God evoked tears of joy and gratitude—these are the times I've felt most touched by His love. For me, these times when I felt so loved and cared for best embody the nature of God. It does not surprise me, then, that He asks us to respond to His love with love: love for God and love for our neighbors. When the Pharisees asked, "Teacher, which is the great commandment in the Law?" Jesus replied, "'You shall love the Lord your God with all your heart, and with all your soul, and with all your mind.' This is the first and greatest commandment. And the second is similar. 'Love your neighbor as yourself'" (Matt. 22:36–39).

I have said that God is love, but what can we know about that love? For me, these three familiar adjectives best express the level and reach of God's pervasive love: *omniscient, omnipresent*, and *omnipotent*. My encounters with God provide clear evidence of these characteristics of God's love.

God's love is *omniscient*; He who is love is all-knowing. God possesses an unbounded, infinite, all-encompassing knowledge and wisdom about everything. With respect to mortal humans, God knows our thoughts, our feelings, our desires, and our needs.

God knew what my depressed son needed to see and hear when we visited a remote and primitive African village. He knew that a reunion with my long-lost friend Warren would provide the impetus I needed to retire early and firmly direct my energies to His work. And he knew many decades earlier that during an unplanned adventure in Poland I would someday stand at the altar at which my maternal grandfather had been baptized as an infant.

Many of my own life stories demonstrate God's omniscient love. The words of the Psalmist in Psalm 139:1–6 ring true to me:

> *You have searched me, LORD,*
> *and you know me.*
> *You know when I sit and when I rise;*
> *you perceive my thoughts from afar.*
> *You discern my going out and my lying down;*
> *you are familiar with all my ways.*
> *Before a word is on my tongue*
> *you, LORD, know it completely.*
> *You hem me in behind and before,*
> *and you lay your hand upon me.*
> *Such knowledge is too wonderful for me,*
> *too lofty for me to attain.*

God's love is *omnipresent*; He who is love is able to be everywhere at all times. This is a concept none of us can fully understand or comprehend because of our own finite boundaries in space and time. It is another of the great mysteries and curiosities surrounding the wonders of God. And by faith I believe it is through the power of the indwelling Holy Spirit that God is present within us always.

I felt God's presence through the guiding influence of the Holy Spirit in the gift of the right words at the right time when I attempted to convince Congressman Sam Johnson of the value of admitting China to the World Trade Organization. The Spirit was with me, protecting me, when I was crouched in the girls' locker room shower stall, camera in hand, and needed to make a potentially life-altering decision in a split second. And the Spirit came to me and my daughter Dena in Seoul, Korea, and led us to the discovery of her ancestral roots.

I rejoice in the omnipresence of God with the Psalmist in Psalm 139:7–12:

Where can I go from your Spirit?
Where can I flee from your presence?
If I go up to the heavens, you are there;
if I make my bed in the depths, you are there.
If I rise on the wings of the dawn,
if I settle on the far side of the sea,
even there your hand will guide me,
your right hand will hold me fast.
If I say, "Surely the darkness will hide me
and the light become night around me,"
even the darkness will not be dark to you;
the night will shine like the day,
for darkness is as light to you.

Finally, God's love is *omnipotent*; He who is love has infinite power to create and to alter. The creator of the universe and all of its diverse life forms has the power even to act in opposition to natural laws and to intervene in miraculous ways on behalf of His faithful believers. Thus, the God who created the universe can also part the Red Sea, walk on water, heal the lame, restore sight to the blind, and even return to life those who have perished.

I was reminded of God's omnipotent power of creation when I saw a beating human heart in New Delhi, India. I personally witnessed His healing powers in the curing of my own migraine headaches. I saw his omnipotence in the miraculous conception and birth of my two sons and in the unexpected healing of my mother's blocked arteries.

I am often reminded of the succinct but powerful statement made by Jesus to the disciples in Matthew 19:26 when He said, "With man this is impossible, but with God all things are possible."

And so, the best way I can find to describe the nature of God is one of *omniscient, omnipresent,* and *omnipotent* love.

Responding to God

As happened to me, you may now realize there have been times in your life when God was delivering a message or providing guidance to you, even though you may have missed it at the time. Moreover, recognizing His involvement now and preparing to hear from Him in the future may already have led you to an important question: *When God speaks, how might I respond?*

If you believe, as I do, that the Holy Spirit of God dwells within you, you can be assured that God is omnipresent in your life. By speaking to God daily in prayer, you will be prepared to hear from Him and to be enriched by His nurture and guidance. I hope you will become more and more attuned to the messages He may be delivering through the providential experiences of your life. As you search out your own blessed encounters with God, I'm confident you can realize a deeper, more enriching relationship with Him.

What do I see as an appropriate response to God? As my relationship with God has deepened through daily prayer and through the recognition of His abiding presence in my life, I have first and foremost expressed my gratitude for His loving and nurturing guidance and presence. In every one of the thirty-one encounters related in this book, I have thanked God profusely for His role in the experience—even those times when it was only later that I realized God had been involved. Even when my response is delayed, I continue to thank Him for the role He played in those events.

We are reminded many times in Scripture of the importance of our thankfulness to God. Two of my favorite verses in the Bible, one in Psalm 107 and the other in Paul's letter to the Colossians, reinforce my earlier conclusions about the nature of God, our preparedness to hear from Him, and how we can respond.

Devote yourselves to prayer, being watchful and thankful.

Colossians 4:2

Give thanks to the LORD, for he is good;
his love endures forever.

Psalm 107:1

In thinking about the appropriate response to God's messages, I am reminded of those stories in the Bible in which God calls on someone whom God has chosen for a purpose, and that chosen believer answers God's call with a simple, "Here I Am!" This moment, a moment of complete openness to God and a willingness to present oneself to be used by the Holy Spirit in any way God desires, is an exemplary response that has inspired Christians for centuries.

In one of these stories of faithful response, Abraham, who has been told by God Himself that his offspring will become God's own chosen people, is prepared to make the most gut-wrenching sacrifice imaginable as God commands him to make a burnt offering of his only son, Isaac (Genesis 22:1–12). When God calls, "Abraham!" Abraham answers simply "Here I am!" And when he receives God's instruction to slaughter his own beloved son as an offering, that "Here I am" guides his obedience as he prepares the sacrifice. His radical faithfulness is rewarded when at the last possible moment, God intervenes to spare Isaac.

In another example in Genesis 46, the Bible tells us that God visited Jacob in a dream. When God calls, "Jacob! Jacob!" Jacob, like his grandfather, responds with a simple "Here I am." In this case, God brings Jacob a word of comfort to allay any fears he might have about going down into Egypt where his son Joseph had been a slave. God tells Jacob not to be afraid and reassures him, "I will make of you a great nation there." With God's promise in his ear, Jacob goes down into Egypt with all his family where they are reunited with his long-lost son Joseph, welcomed by Pharaoh himself, and given the best land in all of the kingdom to settle.

A third biblical example of God's call and the faithful "Here I Am" happens in 1 Samuel 3, after we are told that "the word of the Lord was rare in those days; visions were not widespread." Because of that, the boy Samuel is called several times before he realizes that it is God who is calling. Nevertheless, each time he awakens and hears his name, Samuel responds with "Here I am!" Young Samuel's response is a sign of his readiness to be used by God, and in return, God chooses Samuel as His prophet, entrusting him with the gift of prophecy and the anointing of Israel's first kings.

It is inspiring but difficult for many of us to envision this level of faithfulness and responsiveness to God, but these biblical characters help us to see the ideal response to God's call and to His revelations in our lives. They are the faithful who, without knowing yet what God had in store for them, heard Him call them by name and answered enthusiastically "Here I Am!" It is therefore by their example that when I pray I often say, "Lord, here I am. Use me as you will to serve in your kingdom."

And Finally . . .

In recognizing God's omnipresent, omniscient, and omnipotent love, you can take comfort in knowing that He is with you always, all-knowing and all-powerful in expressing His love. This has been true in your past, it is true now, and I am confident it will be even more evident to you in the future.

By your faithfulness, your prayerfulness, and your watchfulness, you will be well prepared to encounter God in many ways, and your future will be enriched as a result. As you encounter God, express your gratitude by giving thanks for His blessings and His role in your life. But most importantly, let God know that you are on this earth to serve Him and to utilize your unique spiritual gifts in whatever way He leads you. Be prayerful in discerning His will for your life, and be receptive to His calling and His divine guidance. And then give yourself over to Him completely by declaring to Him—as so many biblical characters have in the past and as I do daily—"Here I am."

ABOUT THE AUTHOR

Fred Sievert started his career as a teacher, later entered the insurance business, and retired early—in 2007—as president of New York Life Insurance Company, a Fortune 100 corporation. Feeling he had neglected his spiritual education and development, Fred enrolled in Yale Divinity School where he earned a master's degree in religion in May 2011. His passion is to impact other lives, and to that end he writes, teaches business school courses on strategy and leadership, and serves on the boards of five nonprofit organizations and two for-profit corporations. He also mentors young executives and speaks frequently to church and corporate leaders on the topic of business and spirituality.

Though Fred was not raised in an overtly Christian family, he found God through various life experiences that started in adolescence. This foundation guided and often moderated his aggressive pursuit of business success and the American dream. The power of the stories in God Revealed—and the extent to which God was with Fred throughout his young life and business career—only became fully apparent to him after retirement, as he reflected on his life, his family, and his successes. His stories of encounters with God have been published in numerous printed and electronic periodicals, attracting a large audience of believers, many of whom in turn have shared their own realizations triggered by the work.

CPSIA information can be obtained at www.ICGtesting.com
Printed in the USA
BVOW03s1129030114

340849BV00004B/213/P